PETERSON'S

Game Plan for Getting into

Business School

Michele F. Kornegay

Peterson's
Thomson Learning™

Australia • Canada • Denmark • Japan • Mexico
New Zealand • Philippines • Puerto Rico • Singapore
Spain • United Kingdom • United States

About Peterson's

Founded in 1966, Peterson's, a division of Thomson Learning, is the nation's largest and most respected provider of lifelong learning online resources, software, reference guides, and books. The Education Supersite^{SM} at petersons.com—the Web's most heavily traveled education resource—has searchable databases and interactive tools for contacting U.S.-accredited institutions and programs. CollegeQuest^{SM} (CollegeQuest.com) offers a complete solution for every step of the college decision-making process. GradAdvantage^{TM} (GradAdvantage.org), developed with Educational Testing Service, is the only electronic admissions service capable of sending official graduate test score reports with a candidate's online application. Peterson's serves over 55 million education consumers annually.

Thomson Learning is among the world's largest providers of lifelong learning information. Headquartered in Stamford, CT, with multiple offices worldwide, Thomson Learning is a division of The Thomson Corporation (TTC), one of the world's leading information companies. TTC operates mainly in the U.S., Canada, and the UK and has annual revenues of over US$6 billion. The Corporation's common shares are traded on the Toronto, Montreal, and London stock exchanges. For more information, visit TTC's Internet address at www.thomcorp.com.

Visit Peterson's Education Center on the Internet (World Wide Web) at www.petersons.com

ISBN 0-7689-0392-0

Printed in Canada

10 9 8 7 6 5 4 3 2 1

Acknowledgments

Many people contributed in numerous ways to this project, and I owe them all my gratitude. I must thank the admissions directors who are highlighted in Chapter 6, as well as Karin Nobile of Yale University, who took time from their busy schedules to provide sage words of advice to our readers. Thanks also to the business school students who are featured in Chapter 7; I realize how valuable their time is, and I'm grateful to them for taking a break from their busy schedules to complete my questionnaire. I owe much to Cynthia Ceres and Gary Lynn—a treasured old friend and a wonderful new one—for giving me personal insight into the life of business students; I appreciate their help and, moreover, their friendship.

This book would not have been possible without my fabulous husband, Dan, and the support and encouragement of my mother, Chris, my father, Ed, my stepmother, Elke, and everyone else in the Fetterolf, Evans, Kornegay, and Deitrich families. I truly appreciate everything all of you have given me throughout this long process. Finally, I dedicate this book to Eleanor Lessig, a world-class writer in her own right and my inspiration.

Contents

Contents

Introduction

If you're thinking of applying to one of the more than 900 institutions around the world that offer advanced studies in the field of business, you're not alone. The number of students receiving master's degrees in business is growing every year. From 1970 to 1995, according to the National Center for Education Statistics (NCES), the number of men and women receiving master's degrees in business rose from nearly 26,000 to over 93,000—that's more than a threefold increase! The rise

Graduate Degrees Awarded by Field, 1995–1996, as Percentage of Total Degrees Awarded

Field	Number of Degrees Awarded	Percentage of Total*
Biological sciences	9,151	3%
Public administration and services	17,941	6%
Physical sciences	18,671	6%
Other[†]	20,322	6.5%
Health sciences	22,242	7%
Social sciences	21,754	7%
Engineering	26,333	8.5%
Business	56,284	18%
Education	75,734	24%

*Because not all institutions responded to all items, total percentage does not equal 100.
[†]Other includes architecture, communications, home economics, library sciences, and religion.
Adapted from the Council of Graduate Schools

in doctoral degrees awarded in business studies is also impressive. In 1970–1971, 757 doctoral degrees were awarded in business management and administrative services; in recent years that number topped 1,400. Business is one of the largest fields of master's degree–level study, second only to education in the number of students applying, enrolling, and graduating every year. While business still lags behind education in the number of master's degrees conferred each year, it is quickly catching up and will undoubtedly take the lead in the near future.

Although the number of programs offering advanced study in business has grown over the years to meet this demand, getting into one of the *top-tier* business programs has never been tougher. According to the CGS/GRE Survey of Graduate Enrollment, a joint project of the Council of Graduate Schools and the Graduate Record Examinations Board, in fall 1997, over 135,000 students applied to graduate business programs at the more than 600 institutions in their survey. Recent data from Career Advisor Associates showed that of the 20,000 or more applications received by the top five business programs in the United States, only 3,250, or barely 16 percent, were accepted; the top twenty programs rejected a whopping 80 percent of their applicants. In fall 1997, according to findings of the CGS/GRE survey, 54 percent of applicants to graduate programs in business (over 70,000) were not accepted. To make matters more difficult, from 1986 to 1997, the number of applicants to graduate business programs *increased* by 3 percent, thus narrowing your chances of making the cut.

Graduate Program Acceptance Rates, by Field, Fall 1996

Field	Percentage of Applications Accepted
Biological sciences	29%
Social sciences	32%
Health sciences	36%
Humanities	37%
Physical sciences	40%
Business	46%
Engineering	47%
Other*	54%
Public administration	58%
Education	65%

*Other includes architecture, communications, home economics, library sciences, and religion.
Adapted from the Council of Graduate Schools

ADVANCED DEGREES IN BUSINESS

But let's not get ahead of ourselves. Before we get down to the nitty-gritty of showing you how you can beat the odds and increase your chances of getting into a top postbaccalaureate business program, we should explain exactly what kinds of degrees we're talking about in this book. For our purposes, advanced studies in business include programs that award a wide variety of degrees, including the following:

- Master of Business Administration (M.B.A.) degree, including specialization in many fields, such as media management, professional accounting, public management, quality management, aviation management, international business, decision sciences, economics, computer information systems, executive management, finance, international finance, marketing, taxation, organizational behavior and development, arts management, and health systems administration

- Master of Arts (M.A.) degrees in fields such as organizational management, business and policy studies, and economics
- Master of Science (M.S.) degrees in accounting, finance, banking, statistics, taxation, operations research, marketing, industrial organizational psychology, computer information systems, management systems, human resource development and management, leadership, strategic management, labor relations, telecommunications, computing management, international business, technology management, transportation management, media management, and others
- Executive M.B.A. (E.M.B.A.) degree
- Master of Accounting (M.Acc.) degree
- Master of Taxation and Accounting (M.Tax. A.) degree
- Master of Public Administration (M.P.A.) degree
- Master of Project Management (M.P.M.) degree
- Master of Management (M.Mgt.) degree
- Master of Organizational Development (M.O.D.) degree
- Master of Economics (M.Econ.) degree
- Master of International Management (M.I.M.) degree
- Master of Science in Organizational Management (M.S.O.M.) degree
- Doctor of Philosophy (Ph.D.) degrees in business fields, such as economics
- Dual-degree and or degree plus certification programs, such as those granting the M.B.A./J.D. (Doctor of Jurisprudence), M.B.A./C.P.A (Certified Public Accountant), M.B.A./M.P.H. (Master of Public Health), M.B.A./Ed.D. (Doctor of Education), M.B.A./M.I.A. (Master of International Affairs), M.B.A./M.E. (Master of Engineering), M.B.A./M.I.L.R. (Master of Industrial and Labor Relations), M.B.A./M.Arch. (Master of Architecture), M.B.A./M.D. (Doctor of Medicine), among others, or any number of programs offering joint M.B.A./M.S. and M.B.A./M.A. degrees

This is just the tip of the iceberg. You can enroll in full-time programs, part-time programs, accelerated one-year programs, two-year programs, summer programs, weekend programs, evening programs, and even 48-hour and 64-hour programs. To find a complete listing of all the advanced business degrees that you could possiblyu obtain, take a look at a book like Peterson's *MBA Programs*. You'll be truly amazed at the choices available to you.

SCHOOLS OFFERING BUSINESS PROGRAMS

As we pointed out at the beginning of this chapter, more than 900 institutions of higher learning around the world offer postbaccalaureate programs in business fields. Because advanced study in business is so popular, the types of schools offering these courses of study run the gamut from small private colleges with business schools enrolling only a few hundred students to large state schools whose student bodies can number in the tens of thousands. You can enroll at an Ivy League college or at your hometown university. These days, you can even join the increasing number of students who take distance learning courses from their own home or attend a "virtual university," where opportunities for learning are shared over the Internet. If you're already employed, perhaps your company is one of the increasing number of firms that offer on-site business courses in cooperation with local colleges. The choices are limitless.

WHO GOES TO BUSINESS SCHOOL?

The face of the business school student has dramatically changed over the years. These days, the average business student is not a new college graduate; most have had several years of work experience. Many do not have undergraduate degrees in business. More than half attend part-time. And where thirty years ago the typical business school student was white and male, these days students from all backgrounds enroll in and complete graduate education in business.

Women

More and more women are enrolling in business school and receiving degrees: In a 1996 survey by the International Association for Management Education (AACSB), women comprised almost 34 percent of the student body enrolled in full-time M.B.A. programs and nearly 38 percent of students enrolled in part-time M.B.A. programs. NCES statistics show that in 1970, just 1,010 of the 25,977 students receiving master's degrees in business and 21 of the 757 students receiving doctoral degrees were women; that's a mere 3.8 and 2.8 percent, respectively. But by the mid-1990s those numbers had grown to 34,700 out of 93,809 for master's degrees and 380 out of 1,394 doctoral degrees, a jump to 37 and 27 percent, respectively. Moreover, AACSB noted that the average GPAs for women and men in these programs are virtually identical.

Minority Students

Minority enrollment in graduate business education is also up. According to data from the CGS/GRE Survey of Graduate Enrollment, of all African Americans enrolled in graduate study in fall 1996, 13 percent were enrolled in business programs; American Indians, 11 percent; Asians, 18 percent; Hispanic/Latinos, 12 percent; and whites, 15 percent. From 1986 to 1996, the survey shows, African American enrollment in graduate business education increased 6 percent; American Indian enrollment, 4 percent; Asian enrollment, 9 percent; and Hispanic/Latino enrollment, 6 percent. For the year 1994–1995, according to NCES, 5,165 African American, 2,590 Hispanic, 4,924 Asian/Pacific Islander, and 311 American Indian/Alaskan Native students received master's degrees in business fields.

International Students

AACSB data also show that a growing number of international students are enrolling in full-time and part-time M.B.A. programs—in their survey, more than 24 percent of full-time and nearly 10 percent of part-time students are international.

TRENDS IN GRADUATE ENROLLMENT IN BUSINESS PROGRAMS

While the number of students being awarded undergraduate degrees in business has been dropping since the early 1990s, according to AACSB, the number of M.B.A. degrees awarded in 1995–1996 reached its highest level ever: 93,982. That same year, 1,368 students received doctoral degrees in business; 394 of these degrees were awarded to women. While enrollment in graduate education has declined overall in most fields since the mid-1990s, enrollment in graduate programs in business has increased and held steady over these same years. Enrollment in graduate programs in engineering, social sciences, biological sciences, and humanities has gone down at least 5 percent since 1995; graduate enrollment in physics programs has decreased an astonishing 22 percent since 1992. Meanwhile, enrollment in graduate business programs has increased over the earlier years cited here and has held steady over the past two. According to the CGS, those fields that fared the best in graduate enrollment during the recent downturn share "a close connection between education and subsequent careers." Apparently, the future looks bright for those with advanced degrees in business.

> The average business student is *not* a new college graduate.

BUT WHY SHOULD I GO TO BUSINESS SCHOOL IN THE FIRST PLACE?

Confused? The number of degrees being offered by all those schools is mind-boggling, and with more and more students from all walks of life applying to business programs each year, the competition to get into the best schools is fierce. Wouldn't it be much easier to be content with an undergraduate degree?

Definitely not, and we'll tell you why. Simply put, men and women with advanced degrees have more earning potential. The more education you get, the more money you'll make—it's that easy. According to the March 1998 Current Population Survey released by the U.S. Census Bureau, those with doctoral degrees earn an average of $77,445 per year; those with master's degrees, $51,183; and those with bachelor's degrees, $40,478. With an M.B.A., M.S., or Ph.D. degree on your resume, you'll have more leverage with potential employers when it comes time to discuss your salary. If you go back for an advanced degree while you're already employed, your bosses surely will be impressed by your efforts—and that can only mean good things when your next review comes up.

Projected data by the Bureau of Labor Statistics (BLS) for the years 1996–2006 also paint a rosy picture for those in the field of business, showing an astounding growth rate for management jobs of all types. For example, the BLS Education Level Report shows that by the year 2006, there will be positions for 14.6 percent more general managers and top executives; 18.3 percent more financial managers; 28.5 percent more marketing, advertising, and public relations managers; 11.3 percent more administrative services managers; 21.2 percent more management analysts; a whopping 45.2 percent more engineering, science, and computer systems managers; and 20.5 percent more managers and administrators in other areas. In every category, the number of unemployed and part-time workers in these fields is expected to be very low or low. Data released in November 1998 show that

The Ten Industries with the Fastest Wage and Salary Employment Growth, 1998–2008

Industry	Employment		Change	
	1998	**2008**	**Number**	**Percent**
Computer and data processing services	1,599*	3,472	1,872	117
Health services, not elsewhere classified	1,209	2,018	809	67
Residential care	747	1,171	424	57
Management and public relations	1,034	1,500	466	45
Personnel supply services	3,230	4,623	1,393	43
Miscellaneous equipment rental and leasing	258	369	111	43
Museums, botanical and zoological gardens	93	131	39	42
Research and testing services	614	861	247	40
Miscellaneous transportation services	236	329	94	40
Security and commodity brokers	645	900	255	40

*Numbers in thousands of jobs.
From the Bureau of Labor Statistics

The Ten Occupations with the Largest Job Growth, 1998-2008

Occupation	Employment		Change	
	1998	2008	Number	Percent
Systems analysts	617	1,194*	577	94
Retail salespersons	4,056	4,620	563	14
Cashiers	3,198	3,754	556	17
General managers and top executives	3,362	913	551	16
Truck drivers, light and heavy	2,970	3,463	493	17
Office clerks, general	3,021	3,484	463	15
Registered nurses	2,079	2,530	451	22
Computer support specialists	429	869	439	102
Personal care and home health aides	746	1,179	433	58
Teacher assistants	1,192	1,567	375	31

*Numbers in thousands of jobs.
From the Bureau of Labor Statistics

management and public relations will be the industry with the fourth-fastest predicted wage and salary growth from 1998 to 2008. These same data predict that general managers and top executives will enjoy the fourth-largest occupational growth from 1998 to 2008.

If you've got an entrepreneurial rather than a corporate spirit, think of how much more likely it is that your business will succeed if you've got the solid grounding in business theories and practice that can come only from an advanced education. In fact, many graduating business students have gone on to start their own businesses rather than enter the corporate world. If you dream of being your own boss, the future could be very good to you: BLS data predict that, by the year 2006, more than 45 percent of management analysts will be self-employed, as will more than 52 percent of managers and administrators in miscellaneous areas. When all is said and done, then, you should think of an advanced degree like money in the bank—or, rather, in a high-yield investment account.

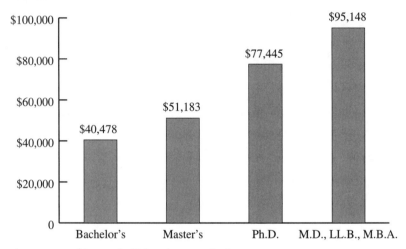

Average annual income, by highest degree attained.

From: "Educational Attainment in the United States," U.S. Bureau of the Census, 1997.

IS GRADUATE SCHOOL RIGHT FOR ME?

The prestige, success, and money that can come with an advanced degree in business sound appealing, to say the least. You're probably imagining yourself as the CEO of that Fortune 500 company right now, aren't you? *Rising to the top of the heap in corporate America. Flying off to exotic locations in your private jet to seal the deal. Your face on the cover of* Forbes *magazine. Taking conference calls with Bill Gates. Retiring to your own private island in the South Pacific . . .*

Now hold on a minute. We hate to burst your bubble, but before you start spending all that money you plan on making, you need to ask yourself a very important question: Do I really have what it takes to get through graduate school?

If you think graduate school is just like college—only a little bit harder—you've made your first mistake. According to Lesli Mitchell, author of *The Ultimate Grad School Survival Guide*, there's a great deal of difference between these two worlds. In graduate school, you're expected to be more independent. Chances are that there won't be anybody looking over your shoulder to make sure you're keeping up. You'll be in charge of choosing your course work. You'll need to learn how to discipline yourself to do the research required for graduate work—and there's a lot of that. You'll need to keep track of your own finances, too, unless your parents are really indulgent or your employer agrees to pay for your schooling. Figuring out how you'll pay for graduate school is one of the first independent steps you'll probably have to take. If you're considering going back for an advanced business degree after several years in the working world, you'll need to get adjusted to the extra time you'll have to spend on studies, since you're probably going to continue working while you get your degree. If you're married and have children, how will you juggle all of these responsibilities? It's something you need to consider seriously.

In graduate school, you'll be required to hone your chosen course of study to an area of specialization. Even if you were an undergraduate business or economics major, you didn't spend all of your class time in business or economics courses. You probably took electives to round out your semesters and provide interesting sidebars to your education. As a master's or doctoral student, you live and breathe your field of study. Think about whether you have what it takes to spend countless hours pouring over Asian banking trends, marketing strategies in the technology sector, or some other specialized area of study, for example. Depending on the business school you attend, you may even need to write a dissertation to receive your degree. Mitchell suggests that you go to the library and check out random titles related to your field in *Dissertation Abstracts*. Can you honestly see yourself performing such specialized research?

Maybe you think that graduate school is the perfect place for you because you were the best undergraduate business or marketing student at your university. You received lots of honors as an undergraduate, so it's only natural to assume that you'll be at the top of the heap in graduate school, too. Unfortunately, grad school is full of "A" students. It makes sense that only the brightest students want to attend and get

> **As a master's or doctoral student, you live and breathe your field of study.**

accepted to programs of advanced study, so as a graduate student you'll be judged by a much higher standard. There will be a lot of competition for grades, grants, scholarships, and other kudos. If you're just out of college, many of your fellow business students will already have years of work experience—and real-world knowledge—under their belts. If you've been working for a few years or more, you won't be as up on the current research trends in the field as recent graduates will be. Either way, you'll need to do a certain amount of catching up. If you want to succeed as a graduate student, you need to take an honest look at your desire and ability to do this.

Finally, graduate students need to learn how to "play the game," so to speak. As Mitchell points out, one of the biggest shocks for incoming graduate students is learning that postbaccalaureate study has a lot to do with politics. Faculty members form alliances and maneuver behind the scenes to control (or try to control) what's going on in the department. Of course, you never saw this as an undergraduate, but once you're a grad student, you'll be privy to all these goings-on. Whom you choose to ally yourself with could make your life easy—or very difficult. Will you be able or even want to deal with such political tensions? This can be very disillusioning for the naive graduate student.

Obviously, then, the first and most important step toward applying to any graduate program is to take a good look at yourself—your personality, your interests, your abilities, and your plans for the future. Don't enroll in a graduate business program solely to make more money. You must be dedicated, interested, and motivated to succeed in any course of graduate study. You'll put in a lot of hours before you get any kind of payoff, so make sure this is something you really want to do.

> **Don't enroll in a graduate business program solely to make more money. You'll put in a lot of hours before you get any kind of payoff, so make sure this is something you really want to do.**

HOW THIS BOOK CAN HELP YOU

Once you've decided that you really want to go to business school, the next steps are to decide which program is right for you and to apply. That's what we're here for. In this book, we'll take you step-by-step through the application and acceptance process.

In Chapter 2, we'll talk about when the right time to think about business school may be for you. If you're currently enrolled in college, would it be better to continue on to graduate school immediately, or is taking a few years off to get experience in the job force a better idea? If you're still in college, we'll discuss what courses you should be taking before you graduate to make sure you've got the background that admissions officers look for. If you've already graduated—a few years ago or several years ago—we'll let you know what refresher courses you may need to get under your belt to get accepted. We'll tell you whom you should turn to with questions about business school so you're sure to have the whole scoop before you apply. And finally, we'll discuss the dreaded Graduate Management Admission Test (GMAT), and what you can do to get the best possible score.

In Chapter 3, you'll begin your search for the business program that best suits your needs. We'll tell you where to gather information about business programs and how to identify the best match for you based on a number of criteria: admissions standards, location, full-time versus part-time options, size, tuition, faculty, specialized programs, job placement, and more. We'll guide you in picking those programs that will help you meet your goals. Then we'll take you through the campus visit. What should you look for? How many schools should you visit? How will you survive that all-important admissions interview? We've got the answers.

Chapter 4 takes you step-by-step through the application and acceptance process. We'll discuss the elements of the application, with special emphasis on essays, and will give you tips on how to stay organized through this often daunting process. We'll also tell you all you need to know about GradAdvantage, the easy way to apply to graduate school. Once the acceptance letters start rolling in, the tips you'll find here will help you decide which program you want to attend.

Now that you've applied and been accepted to a graduate business program, you need to figure out how you're going to pay for it. Chapter 5 discusses the many options available to you, from scholarships to government and private loans. We'll talk about federal, state, local, and private sources of aid, as well as aid offered by the individual schools themselves. If you're already working, we'll tell you how to find out whether your company will pay for your education while you work part-time. And we'll consider several resources that are out there to help you find financial aid.

In Chapter 6, you'll get advice from business school admissions directors and counselors themselves. What are they *really* looking for when they review your application? What can you do to make yourself stand out from the crowd? How much does your GMAT score really matter, anyway? You'll get the answers to these and other questions posed to admissions personnel across the country.

In Chapter 7, "Advice from Business School Students," business school students and graduates candidly discuss their experiences with applying to business school. Their words of advice could make your life much easier and help you avoid the most common pitfalls that can befall business school applicants.

Chapter 8 discusses an option you may want to consider when choosing a graduate program in business: studying for your degree at a college or university outside the United States. In the global marketplace of the twenty-first century, such a degree could take you far in your business career. We'll tell you all you need to know about picking the right program if you think studying overseas might be right for you.

Finally, the appendixes at the end of the book provide you with an in-depth application timeline and list resources to help you along your journey.

We hope you'll use this book to pave the way toward a bright future in the business world. Be confident, and go get 'em!

Getting Started

Once you've made the decision to apply to business school, you'll need to begin the planning process. In this chapter, we'll discuss the initial steps you should take before you begin gathering information about schools and applying to them.

THINKING ABOUT YOUR FUTURE

Probably more than most graduate fields of study, business programs are, for the most part, tailored to students who hope to have specific careers. If you know you want to be in a business field but aren't quite sure exactly what you want to be doing or where you want to be working in the years to come, the first thing you'll need to do is some serious soul-searching about your career and your future. Before you even begin gathering information about programs, you need to know just what it is that you want to get out of the program you'll enter. Obviously, there's a great deal of difference in the training you'll receive in an advanced program with an emphasis on marketing versus an advanced program focused on finance. Because of the specialized nature of most graduate degree programs in business, you'll be doing yourself a great disservice if you enroll in any one just to get an advanced degree. Remember, future employers will hire you for positions based on the degree you receive. If you're not sure you want to work in a specific profession—say, labor relations—upon graduating from business school, by all means, don't enroll in that kind of program in the first place.

Furthermore, knowing exactly what you want to get out of business school will affect your status in the eyes of admissions directors. If you have clear goals and objectives and state them succinctly on your admissions application, you'll be looked at more favorably than someone who simply states that he is "interested in business." According to the Graduate Management Admission Council (GMAC), "The strongest candidates competing to gain admission into graduate business school are very focused on their intended career paths." As they point

Game Plan for Getting into Business School

Chapter 2

Is a Business Degree Right for You? Ask Yourself These Questions:

- Why am I interested in a degree in business?
- What interests do I plan to pursue with a degree in business?
- How can a degree in business help me achieve my goals?
- Without an advanced degree in business, will I have to modify my goals?
- What are my strengths?
- What are my weaknesses?
- What personal factors should I consider (family, lifestyle, financial)?
- What is important to me—job satisfaction, security/income, lifestyle? How do these priorities affect one another and my desire to pursue advanced studies in business?
- Do I feel strongly about a certain area of business? Why?
- What is the evidence that a business degree is the next logical step for me?
- Am I ready to be a student again? Do I have the commitment and the discipline?
- Do I have the financial means to go to school full-time, or should I pursue studies part-time?

out, the length of most advanced business programs (one or two years) is too short to help you *discover* an affinity for a particular profession. Therefore, admissions counselors want to see evidence on your application that you are confident in your professional interests.

If you're already in the workplace or know what your career goals are, you may want to think about whether or not you need an advanced degree to get ahead in your field. Talk to people who already have the job you want. How did they get there? Did they need a graduate degree to land their job, or could a variety of routes lead to your ideal career? You may find that taking targeted courses, getting more training or supervision through your employer, or using your connections to enter a field or organization and move up may be easier than—and just as effective as—getting a business degree. Also, think about whether or not you're willing to accept the responsibilities that those with advanced business degrees must face once they're in the job force. As the GMAC points out, those with M.B.A.s are accountable for employees, budgets, deadlines, major accounts, and other huge responsibilities. Their higher ncome carries with it more risks and their employers expect them to produce stellar work and put in demanding hours. Do you want to succeed in your chosen field enough to subject yourself to this?

This thinking and decision process is be one of the most difficult tasks you face as you embark on your search for a business school. You may want to take several aptitude and interests inventories, such as the Learning Styles Inventory or the Myers-Briggs Type Inventory, or read books like *What Color Is Your Parachute?* by Richard Nelson Bolles and other career advice/self-assessment books. You can also check out the GMAC's Web site, www.gmat.org, which includes a Pre-MBA Self-Assessment and Planning Worksheet that you can fill in, or request their publication *Exploring the MBA*, which provides you with valuable information about the M.B.A. degree and the M.B.A. admissions process.

Finally, make sure you have support systems in place before you venture off to graduate school. If you're married, are your spouse and children supportive of your decision? Remember, you'll be putting in a lot of extra work to get your degree, whether you go to school part- or full-time. Be sure that your family understands this and that they support you in your efforts. If you are working, your employer must be aware of your decision to attend graduate school and should be willing to make accommodations, if necessary, to help you adapt to your new schedule. Most importantly, get yourself in shape both mentally and physically before you begin this process. The road to a graduate degree isn't easy, so be sure that you're confident and healthy enough to deal with the bumps along the way.

Good planning, which includes self-examination of your strengths, weaknesses, and interests, is the first step toward helping you identify those schools that are best for you. You want to get the best return on your investment in a graduate program, don't you? Having a clear sense of direction regarding your career will go a long way toward making that happen.

> Don't enroll in graduate school as a way to avoid working. Remember—many business programs require more time and effort than a full-time job.

STARTING THE PLANNING PROCESS— A TIMELINE

Investigating and applying to graduate programs can be a time-consuming process. In general, it's safe to allow yourself at least six months to research programs, hone your choices, visit campuses, request letters of recommendation from professors and employers, work on your personal statement, and take the GMATs (and TOEFL, if you're an international student) *before* you even begin the application process.

Most graduate school applicants would benefit from sticking to the following schedule:

Six months prior to applying:

Research areas of interest, institutions, and programs.

Talk to advisers about application requirements.

Register and prepare for appropriate graduate admissions tests.

Investigate national scholarships.

Obtain letters of recommendation.

Request transcripts from all universities you have attended.

Three months prior to applying:

Take required graduate admissions tests (GMAT, TOEFL).

Write for application materials.

Write your application essay.

Check on application deadlines and rolling admissions policies.

Fall, a year before matriculating:

Obtain letters of recommendation.

Take graduate admissions tests, if you haven't already.

Send in completed applications.

Winter, before matriculating in the fall:

Complete the Free Application for Federal Student Aid (FAFSA) and Financial Aid Profile, if required.

Spring, before matriculating in the fall:

Check with all institutions before their deadlines to make sure your file is complete:

Visit institutions that accept you.

Send a deposit to your institution of choice.

Notify other colleges and universities that accepted you of your decision to go elsewhere so that they can admit students on their waiting list.

Send thank-you notes to people who wrote your recommendation letters, informing them of your success.

You may not be able to adhere to this general timetable if application deadlines are very early or if you decide to attend graduate school at the last minute. But be sure to keep in mind all of the various application requirements, and be sure to meet all deadlines. If a deadline is impossible for you to meet, call the institution to see if a late application will be considered. If the school you wish to apply to has rolling admissions—where applications are reviewed on an ongoing basis as they are received—try to act as early as possible. Early application will work in your favor, as it will show your enthusiasm for a program and will give admissions committees more time to evaluate the subjective components of your application. Also, once a program with rolling admissions is full, no more applications are considered, so make sure you don't miss out on a program that you really want to attend by applying too late.

As a quick guide, you can consult Appendix 1 ("Planning and Application Timeline") at the back of this book during the planning and applying stages.

If the school you wish to apply to has rolling admissions—where applications are reviewed on an ongoing basis as they are received—try to act as early as possible.

THE COURSES AND SKILLS YOU'LL NEED TO GET ADMITTED TO BUSINESS SCHOOL

Think that you need to have an undergraduate degree in business to get accepted to business school? Hardly. Turns out that only about half of all M.B.A. students enter business school with a business or economics degree. Therefore, your undergraduate specialization should have little effect on your chances for admission to business school. In fact, if you're still an undergraduate and are considering taking business administration courses before applying to an M.B.A. program, you may want to look at the curricula of some of the graduate programs you're interested in before you do so. Most M.B.A. programs offer or require a core curriculum of basic business courses as part of the graduate degree, so you'll be duplicating your efforts if you take undergraduate business courses.

Business schools look to see if you have certain quantitative skills, however, so if you're an undergraduate liberal arts or sciences major, you may want to have calculus, statistics, accounting, or economics courses on your transcript in preparation for application. If you're already employed and don't have these courses on your transcripts, consider enrolling in a college course before applying. If you took these courses in college some time ago, take the time to review your knowledge of the subject, as some M.B.A. programs require incoming students to pass a basic quantitative test before registering for classes. Make sure you know exactly what skill set is expected before you enroll. To brush up, you may consider using one of the GMAC's Pre-MBA CD-ROMs in finance, accounting, and quantitative skills, available through their M.B.A. store at www.gmat.org.

Many experts also recommend that you learn how to use spreadsheet computer programs, such as Lotus or Excel, before going to business school, as business students—particularly M.B.A. students—probably use spreadsheet programs more than any other type of computer software. At the bare minimum, make sure you are comfortable using spreadsheet software. Install it on your computer, browse the user manual, and practice some simple functions. You should need only a few weeks to get the hang of it. In fact, as more and more businesses are looking for technology-savvy employees, it probably wouldn't hurt to show admissions committees that you have a firm grasp of different aspects of computer technology when you apply.

Admissions directors of business schools look to enroll students who can lead people. In fact, leadership ability will be one of the basic ingredients of your future success in the business world. Your application will be viewed more favorably if you can show that you have leadership experience that includes communication skills, initiative, and the ability to work with and motivate others. For example, if you're an English major and are thinking of applying to a business school, run for president of the school literary society or editor of the campus newspaper. If you're already employed, volunteer to head up projects or organize company events. Having these accomplishments on your application will boost your chances of admission.

Most M.B.A. programs offer or require a core curriculum of basic business courses as part of the graduate degree, so you'll be duplicating your efforts if you take undergraduate business courses.

TO WORK OR NOT TO WORK?
THE VALUE OF WORK EXPERIENCE IN THE
APPLICATION PROCESS

According to most sources, these days, your work history is one of the most crucial aspects of your application to business school. Without work experience, your chances of admission to a top-tier program are basically nonexistent, despite the strengths of the rest of your application. Why do business schools place such emphasis on work experience in reviewing candidates for admission? Simply put, solid experience in the job market shows admissions directors that you are capable of performing in the world of business and provides them with an idea of your potential to complete and succeed at advanced business studies. Schools want to graduate students that they'll be proud to have in the ranks of their alumni—students who will get recruited by top firms or go on to launch successful businesses, which, in turn, will make the school look even better to future potential applicants. Your job experience will also show admissions committees if you've progressed far enough to benefit from a graduate education in business school—or if you've progressed so far that an advanced degree would not be useful to you. Finally, the work experiences you've had show what kind of industry perspective you'll carry with you into graduate school.

The standard for many business programs is for the applicant to have at least two years of work experience. As competition for spots has increased over the past several years, many top programs have begun searching for applicants with three years or more of work experience. When reviewing your work experience, admissions directors look at the reputation of the company or companies for whom you've worked, the diversity of your experience in the marketplace, whether or not you've advanced in your career over time, the caliber of your professional and interpersonal skills, and your potential for leadership.

If you're still in college, don't be discouraged by the news that most business programs look for students who already have work experience. Be sure to check with the programs in which you're interested. Some may not have this requirement, and others may look at a strong college internship experience as an acceptable alternative to

> **Without work experience, your chances of admission to a top-tier program are basically nonexistent, despite the strengths of the rest of your application.**

experience in the job market. If the program to which you want to apply does require a few years of real-world work experience, keep this in mind: If you go out and find a job in the business sector upon graduating from college, chances are that, after a few years of working, your employer will pay for you to attend a graduate business program. As we'll discuss in the next chapter, these days, employers looking to stay competitive are often more than willing to foot the bill for employees with a bright future to return for an advanced business degree. A few years in the job market could help you kill two birds with one stone—getting admitted and paying for business school.

WHERE CAN YOU TURN FOR ADVICE AND INFORMATION?

These days, employers looking to stay competitive are often more than willing to foot the bill for employees with a bright future to return for an advanced business degree.

As you start examining schools, be sure to talk to students enrolled in business programs, admissions officers, and alumni. The more perspectives you have, the more insight you'll gain and the better equipped you'll be to make the right decision about which school you should attend. Students who are currently enrolled in the programs you're interested in or alumni from these programs will provide you with insider information about exactly what you can expect from the program. If you don't know anyone who is currently enrolled or who graduated from the program, contact the school's admissions office, which will be sure to have names of students you can contact. Admissions counselors will also give you invaluable information about every aspect of the program. Be sure to get all the details before you decide to apply.

Even if you don't have a short list of schools yet, talk to current and former business school students and admissions counselors about the overall experience. If you're still in college, sit down with the professors that you respect the most and ask them about the overall graduate school experience and about specific schools and programs. They undoubtedly will have valuable information and words of wisdom to impart. Web surfers can find ample advice and information about business school programs and the business school experience in chat rooms for current and past students or through sites like www.about.com, which features a network of information specifically for business majors.

Colleagues in the workplace can be invaluable resources when you're considering enrolling in business school. Talk to some of the people you work with who already have business degrees. What advice do they have about the selection, application, and admissions processes? Ask them to be honest about how having an advanced degree in business has changed their lives. Would they do it again if they had the chance? How can you learn from the mistakes they feel they may have made? You can also discuss the pros and cons of enrolling in a business program with your supervisor—after all, he or she is in the best position to tell you how obtaining an business school degree could affect your career. Talk to people in the human resources department at your company. What advice can they give you about the benefits of an advanced degree?

You may want to go on informational interviews with professionals in the career field in which you're interested. In an informational interview, you request meetings with industry professionals to get ideas and advice about a specific company or job. In most cases, such men and women are more than happy to share experiences and offer advice; in the process, you'll make valuable contacts that could serve you well later on. According to the GMAC, when you go on an informational interview, your goals are threefold:

1. To determine if the career you are considering still seems interesting to you after learning more about it.

2. To determine if an advanced degree in business is essential or helpful to those in your potential career path.

3. To determine whether a particular type of work experience or internship is important to your career goals.

GMAC advises the following regarding informational interviews:

- Be sure to tell your contacts how you got their names and why you want to talk to them. Point out that you want to meet them to help you determine your compatibility with a specific job or industry and to determine whether a business degree is a logical step to help you enter the field.

> Be sure to find out from people in the field what career responsibilities and advantages you could expect with and without an advanced degree.

- Send a resume in advance so that your contact knows something about you before the meeting. Confirm the meeting time, and don't take more than 30 minutes. Above all, do not ask for a job during your meeting. You are there purely for fact-finding.
- Send a thank-you note after the interview is over. Keep the person posted periodically of your progress.

THE GMAT

Now that you've taken a good look at your career plans, brushed up on the skills that you'll need to succeed in business school, and spoken with students, colleagues, and admissions people about the business school environment and the benefits of obtaining an advanced business degree, it's time to face the dreaded Graduate Management Admission Test—the GMAT.

What Is the GMAT?

Total scoring on the GMAT ranges from 200 to 800.

The GMAT uses a standardized set of criteria which allows graduate schools to compare and judge applicants to evaluate the basic skills of college graduates. The test measures general verbal and math skills so that schools can assess your ability to succeed in a graduate-level environment. The GMAT does not test specific knowledge of business or achievement in a particular subject. The skills that are tested are those that you should have already encountered or developed in your academic career.

The GMAT consists of three sections: a multiple-choice quantitative section, which measures mathematical skills and the ability to solve quantitative problems; a multiple-choice qualitative section, which focuses on verbal skills, the ability to understand and interpret written materials, and basic English writing skills; and the analytical writing assessment, for which you have to write two essays—one about your opinion on an issue and another in which you analyze the reasoning in an argument. Nonstandard testing accommodations, including extended testing time, additional or extended breaks, selectable background and foreground colors, a test reader, a recorder of answers, and a sign language interpreter for spoken directions, are available for test-takers with documented disabilities. Total scoring on the GMAT ranges from

Tips and Tricks to Help You on the GMAT-CAT:

- Understand the directions for each question type before you go in to take the test. This will save you valuable time. Test-prep manuals and other tools will help you with this.

- Take your time with the questions at the beginning of each section. The questions at the beginning of a section affect your score more than those at the end. Once the computer determines your general ability level with these initial questions, you'll be able to improve your score dramatically.

- Be completely sure of each answer before proceeding. Remember, you can't skip a difficult question and return to it later, as you could on the paper test. Nor can you review responses to questions that you have already answered. You must, therefore, be confident about your answer before you confirm it and proceed. If you are totally stumped, eliminate as many answer choices as you can, select the best one, and move on.

- Pace yourself. To finish both sections, you need to establish a pace that allows you to spend, on average, just under 2 minutes per item. So you'll need to work quickly and accurately to complete each section within the 75-minute time constraint.

- Be prepared to receive a mix of different question types within each section. On the paper GMAT, questions were typically grouped by type. On the GMAT-CAT, however, the computer may select one of several question formats, depending on whether you answered the previous question correctly or incorrectly. Be ready for this.

- Use the scratch paper that is provided at the test center. You aren't allowed to bring any paper or other materials into the test center, and since there is no test booklet, you will want to take advantage of the scratch paper that the test center provides. Use it to solve math problems, draw diagrams, or record any other information that helps you work accurately and quickly.

200 to 800. Your basic test registration fee covers the release of your score to up to five graduate schools, which you select at test time. You may request that additional schools receive your scores for an extra fee. For detailed information about the GMAT, you can request the *GMAT Information Bulletin* from the GMAC or download it from their Web site at www.gmat.org.

The GMAT-CAT

As of October 1997, the GMAT has been administered only as a computer-adaptive test, or CAT, which is radically different from the old paper-and-pencil format. On the CAT, questions must be answered in order, so you can't jump ahead to easier questions and save harder ones for later, nor can you go back and change answers, as you could on the paper-and-pencil test. On the CAT, you have to answer every question, so guessing—and knowing how to eliminate incorrect answers—is more important on the new test. But the biggest change is that the CAT is *adaptive*: how well you do on the early questions determines how hard the later questions will be. If you answer the first medium-level question correctly, the computer raises your score and proceeds to give you a harder question. If you answer incorrectly, your score goes down and the next question will be easier. The process repeats for each question in the section. The difficulty of the questions, not just the number you get right, affects your score. With the CAT, you can see your score on the multiple-choice questions before you leave the room, but once you decide to see your score, you can't cancel it, and it gets sent to the schools you requested to receive it. (With the paper test, you had one week to cancel your score so it wouldn't count.)

You need minimal computer skills to take the CAT, and you have plenty of time at the test center to work through a tutorial that allows you to practice answering questions, using the mouse, using the word processor, and accessing the help function. The GMAT-CAT is available year-round at test centers throughout the world.

How to Prepare for the GMAT

You can improve your scores and reduce your anxiety by preparing for the exams you need to take. At the very least, preparation will mean that you are familiar with the test instructions and the types of questions you will be asked. If your computer skills need improvement, adequate preparation will mean you can focus on the questions rather than struggle with the mouse when you take the computer-based tests.

Many students don't trust themselves to stick with a self-study program using practice tests, workbooks, or software (for a sampling of some, check out Appendix 2, "Resources," at the end of this book). If this sounds like you, you may prefer the structure and discipline of a professional review course. Although the courses are much more expensive than the do-it-yourself approach, with fees running upward of $1,000, they may be worth it if they make you study.

Essay Questions

The way the essay portion of the GMAT is graded changed in February 1999 to include the "E-rater," a computer program designed to analyze analytical writing ability. Both the E-rater and a human scorer grade your essays. If the human and the E-rater agree on the grade, that's the score your essay receives. If they disagree, a second human grades the essay to resolve any differences.

How Important Are Your Scores on the GMAT?

While most schools require applicants to submit the result of their GMATs, the importance of the GMAT in admissions varies, depending on the school. Minimum score requirements do not exist at some business schools, and test scores are certainly not the sole criteria for admission to business programs—but to some degree or another, most business schools use them as part of the admissions process. Your score on the GMAT is seen as a "success indicator" for future academic work, and it is used to compare you with other applicants to the school. Top-tier schools like to have applicant pools with high scores; they find that this is an indicator of their prestige and selectivity. However, a good GMAT score may not necessarily get you into the school of your choice, since so many other factors are at play in your application (we'll discuss this more in Chapter 4, "The Application Process"). But a bad score will most certainly keep you out. If your scores are more than 50 points below a school's average, you may be facing an uphill battle, and you should think about retaking the test. Most business schools will focus on your most recent score. You may take the GMAT once in a calendar month.

> Because your essay will be graded by a computer, be sure to set up a logical structure and write in a clear, effective style. This is not the place to be funny or innovative!

THE TOEFL AND OTHER REQUIREMENTS FOR INTERNATIONAL STUDENTS

International students must follow the same application procedures as other graduate students. However, several additional requirements must usually be met. If English is not your native language, you will be required to take the Test of English as a Foreign Language (TOEFL) or a similar test. The TOEFL evaluates the English proficiency of individuals whose native language is not English. Administered under the direction of the Educational Testing Service, the TOEFL is offered as a Computer Adaptive Test in most parts of the world. Some schools may wave the TOEFL requirement if you have studied at or have a degree from a college or university in a country where the native language is English.

In addition to scores on the TOEFL or other proof of English language competence, international student applications must be accompanied by a certified English translation of your academic transcripts. You may also have to submit records of immunization and certain health certificates, as well as documented evidence of financial support, at the time of application. If you are an international student, be sure to request these documents early in the application process.

Now that you've decided that business school is the right step and know about the initial work you need to do before you apply, it's time to find the best business program for you. This is where the really hard work begins—and you thought the GMAT was tough!

If English is not your native language, you will be required to take the Test of English as a Foreign Language (TOEFL) or a similar test.

Picking a School

I hope that the first two chapters of this book have led you to really think about your decision to go to business school. If nothing else, you should have learned that it's not something you want to enter into without total dedication. Now that you've decided that an advanced degree in business is right for you, it's time to do the hard work: choosing the best schools to which you should apply.

Remember, you ultimately want to attend the school that's best for you, not the school that's said to be "the best" by any one of the many rankings lists that you'll find or by your friends and colleagues. In this chapter, we'll discuss some of the criteria to consider when looking at business schools. The first step is to decide which are the most important to you. Then you can see how individual schools meet your requirements. Having a clear sense of what's important to you before you apply will guarantee that your business school experience will be an enjoyable and beneficial one.

GATHERING INFORMATION

Many resources exist to help you gather information about potential schools. You can do research at your local library, in your employer's human resources office, at your undergraduate school, or from the luxury of your own home.

You may want to look at some of the guidebooks out there, such as Peterson's *MBA Programs*. Books like this will give you all the details on degrees awarded, admission requirements, application deadlines, teaching methodologies, facilities, demographics, placement services, costs, financial aid, as well as contact information for every school listed.

If you're already employed in the business sector, go to your employer's human resources office. You'll be sure to find a wealth of information there about business programs in which past and present workers have enrolled. The human resources director will also be able to tell you about programs that are recommended for your particular field and about whether or not your company can help defray the costs of attending.

If you're still an undergraduate, visit your college's guidance or career office, which is sure to be filled with brochures, pamphlets, directories, and all kinds of information about advanced business programs. Guidance personnel will also be happy to sit down with you to discuss the strengths and weaknesses of individual programs, application procedures, and options for financing advanced studies as well as offer encouragement and advice throughout your search.

Internet aficionados can find tons of information about business programs on the Web. A great place to start is www.gradadvantage.org, a Web-based, electronic admissions service developed by the Educational Testing Service (ETS) and Peterson's that also provides detailed information on participating schools. If you decide you're interested in one of the schools found on the site, you can even apply on line! Through the Internet, you can access individual school's Web sites (there's hardly a school out there that doesn't have a Web site) as well as online discussion groups for business students, where you can chat with students who currently enrolled in business programs and receive online newsletters related to the field (about.com has one such forum devoted specifically to business majors).

Using the print and online sources available to you, request brochures and pamphlets directly from the programs in which you're most interested. These materials often contain more information than Web sites and print directories do, and you'll often find that the individual programs themselves are your best source for the most detailed information about curriculum, facilities, faculty, and so on. Materials directly from the schools will also give you the specifics about whom to contact personally for more about application deadlines, financial aid, and other specific pieces of information.

Finally, in gathering information about business programs, don't overlook the value of word of mouth. If you know people who are currently enrolled in business programs or who have already received a business degree, don't be shy about asking for their opinions about the programs they attended. Personal insight into a program is invaluable

Be sure to listen and to weigh each person's experiences carefully if you ask for subjective impressions about business programs.

as you compile your short list of schools. Remember again, however, that one person's opinion is just that—an opinion. Your best friend from high school and your officemate may have graduated from the same business program but have completely different views on the value of that program. Be sure to listen to and to weigh each person's experiences carefully if you ask for subjective impressions about business programs.

STAYING ORGANIZED

With all the information you'll be gathering, staying organized is important. You may want to get a notebook and start a separate page for each program that includes pertinent facts about each school. Or you can photocopy the form at the end of this chapter for easy reference. As you find out more about a school or program in which you're interested, fill in the information in the spaces provided. Above all, be sure to keep track of application deadlines.

IDENTIFYING CRITERIA

Once you've gathered your materials, it's time to start looking at those factors that are important to you. In this section we discuss the most important criteria that you'll want to consider. How you weigh each of these factors is up to you. You may decide that the location of the program that you attend is more important than its cost or that a program's teaching methodology should be given more emphasis than whether or not it offers paid internships. Remember, no one factor in and of itself is more important than any other; the importance comes from what you personally have decided is best for you.

So how do you choose between a full- and a part-time program?

Length of Program

Perhaps the biggest decision you'll have to make is whether to attend business school full- or part-time. If you decide to enroll full-time, you have the choice of attending for two years or for one year. If you enroll in a part-time program, you can choose from evening programs, weekend programs, weeklong intensive programs, summer programs, and distance programs—among other options. Now more than ever, business programs are recognizing that to attract students and stay competitive they have to be more flexible in the types of programs they offer. This is great news for you, but the wide array of choices you'll be confronted with will be awe-inspiring.

So how do you choose between a full- and a part-time program? You'll find many opinions on both sides. If you're already working in a job you like, you probably don't want to leave your job to attend a full-time program—unless, of course, your employer is willing to give you an extended leave of absence. Most full-time business students are considering job changes (or have at least decided to leave the companies they were working for) and have left the work force temporarily to get training for a different career; most part-time students are looking to enhance the careers they already have.

Full-Time Programs

With a full-time program, you know you'll be finished with your studies in a set amount of time—either two years or one year—and you'll be able to reenter the work force at a higher salary that much sooner. You won't have to worry about playing a balancing act between work and school, since your time will be devoted solely to your studies. Campus and program facilities will be completely accessible to you, since most are designed to accommodate "traditional" students. The full-time graduate experience also allows for more interaction between students and faculty members; full-time students go through the experience with a certain sense of togetherness, as they study, attend class, and socialize together and generally have more access to professors and campus facilities. A full-time program provides you with the "face time" that's critical to success in the business world, where you'll be called on to negotiate, work in teams, and communicate face-to-face on a daily basis.

Part-Time Programs

If you think you want to continue working and attend a program part-time, you'll need to weigh a lot of variables. Juggling work, school, and family life can be tough. Ask yourself how much time you have

The full-time graduate experience allows for more interaction between students and faculty members.

realistically to devote to classes and out-of-class studies. Do you work late hours? Do you have many family obligations? Squeezing in a part-time business program probably isn't a good idea if you find yourself in this scenario. If you decide to get your business degree part-time, make sure your employer and your family are behind you. Many employers encourage their workers to get advanced degrees and even pay for business school course work; some, like Ernst & Young, give workers time off in the summer to attend business school part-time; others offer programs on site to help you get your degree.

The good news is that part-time business programs have recognized the many demands that their students face and are becoming more flexible to attract students. More students than ever before are receiving business degrees from part-time programs, and business schools now must cater to these students. In some programs, part-time students have their own financial aid office, career advisers, and evening library hours. To keep students in touch with each other and with professors to form a bond similar to that felt in full-time programs, business schools are taking advantage of technology to keep students and professors wired via e-mail and the Internet to encourage communication. Many part-time programs require that students spend weekends or weeks together in "academic retreats," which encourage them to socialize and build networks of professional contacts.

If you're thinking about a part-time business program, find out if the experience of part-time students is different from that of full-time students. Look at the course lists for both the full-and part-time program: Are the same courses offered for both? Make sure that campus and program facilities and organizations accommodate part-time students. Will the library, technical center, student lounges, and parking lots be open when you need them? Do student organizations meet at a time that's convenient to part-time students? Finally, will your professors be as available to you as a part-time student as they would be if you were a full-time student? Do the same professors teach full- and part-time courses? At some schools, tenured full professors teach in the full-time program, while nontenured adjunct professors teach in part-time students. Does this matter to you?

> If you're considering a part-time program and know you want to stay with the company for which you're currently working, check with your employer first to see what they can do for you.

Some distance programs compensate for the lack of "face time" by requiring students to visit campus a few times a year for mandatory residencies.

Distance Programs

Another option you may want to consider is getting your business degree on line through one of the many distance education programs that are available. The number of distance programs offering advanced degrees in business has grown incredibly over the past few years and will continue to grow as more and more students log on for classes. (For a sampling of M.B.A. distance learning programs, visit www.petersons. com.) A distance program can enable you to attend a school across the country without ever leaving home—or your job. You can even move to another part of the world, travel, or change jobs and still attend the program. You log on when you're ready to learn, from anywhere that there is Internet access, offering students the ultimate in flexibility. Some distance programs compensate for the lack of "face time" by requiring students to visit campus a few times a year for mandatory residencies. All of the programs use the Internet and e-mail to keep students in touch with each other and with faculty members. The curricula in distance programs are just as strenuous as those in full-time or traditional part-time classes, so if you decide to enroll in an online program, make sure you've got the discipline to succeed. You'll need to be able to establish a regular study schedule without being reminded to meet deadlines by instructors or classmates.

Location and Size

When looking at each school's location, decide up front whether you really want to make a big move or not. Making a move that takes you out of your element could confuse you and hinder your studies—or it could be an exciting and welcome change that gives your brain a jump start. If you're married or have a family, be sure to take their feelings on the subject to heart. Consider how the location of the program will affect the overall quality of the graduate school experience. If you've always lived in a rural setting, think long and hard about accepting a position at a school in a large, urban area like New York or Chicago. It may seem exciting, but city life requires a lot of adjustment—to traffic, to noise, and to lots and lots of people. On the other hand, if you're a born and bred city slicker, you will have to adapt to the slower pace of life at a school in a rural location. Life in the "great outdoors" may sound peaceful, but will you freak out if you can't find a slice of pizza at 3 a.m.? With everything else that you're going to have to tackle as a business school student, you may not want to add in the extra stress of changing geographic locations. If you're hoping to eventually work in a specific area of the country, however, going to business school in that area will help you establish contacts in the business community that you'll be able to access once you've received your degree.

Enrollment figures should also be a consideration. Think back to your undergraduate experience. Did the size of the school that you attended affect you positively or negatively? How comfortable were you there? When considering business programs, it's important to look not only at the size of the university as a whole but also at the size of the business program itself and the size of the degree program in which you'll be enrolling. They should be big enough to support an interesting curriculum, but small enough that you can get individual attention, if you need it.

Campus Culture

Try to glean information about the campus and program culture as you read about each school. It may not seem important at first glance whether the university as a whole and the program specifically are more casual than formal, more conservative than liberal, more competitive than cooperative, or more studious than raucous, but it is important that you feel as though you fit in wherever you go. Although graduate students don't get as caught up in the campus lifestyle as undergraduates do, the overall feel of the school will affect you. Moreover, the feel of the business school will be sure to have an impact on you. If you spent your undergraduate and subsequent working years in an environment that was ethnically diverse, make sure that the business school you attend is diverse as well. If you want to be surrounded by friendly faces, cross programs that are known for their cutthroat competitiveness off your list. When all is said and done, you'll be glad you did.

Admissions Criteria and Attrition Rate

You have a fine line to walk when considering admissions criteria. You want to get accepted to the "best" school that meets your needs, of

> **If you're hoping to eventually work in a specific area of the country, however, going to business school in that area will help you establish contacts in the business community that you'll be able to access once you've received your degree.**

course, but you shouldn't be unrealistic about it. Think about how going to a school with a great reputation will promote your career. If you want to enter a field where there's intense competition, you probably want to be admitted to a program that has tougher admissions criteria, which is an indication of its reputation. But think about this, too: a program's admissions criteria and national rankings are probably directly proportional to how tough the program will be. If it's that hard to get into the school, imagine how hard it will be to keep up and do well in the program. And the more competitive it is to get in, the more competitive it will probably be throughout the program. Is that something you think you'll be comfortable with?

Don't be discouraged when you look at a school's stated admissions criteria. Remember that a program's "required" GPAs and GMAT scores only tell part of the story. If your score on the GMAT and your undergraduate GPA fall just below a program's stated criteria, consider applying anyway. As we'll see in the next chapter, other elements of your application can swing an admissions committee's decision in your favor. Likewise with job experience. If the committee says that it wants to see two years of work experience in its candidates but you're an undergraduate who's had two solid summers of an excellent internship in the field, make your case for admission in your application essay (don't worry, we'll show you how to write a fantastic personal statement). You want to be realistic, but there's no reason why you shouldn't apply to your dream school if you fall just slightly below the stated criteria.

Although graduate students don't get as caught up in the campus lifestyle as undergraduates do, the overall feel of the school will affect you.

While looking at a program's admissions criteria, check out its attrition rate as well. How many students who make it into the program actually stay on and receive a degree? This is an important piece of data to have, as a high attrition rate could indicate that many students find serious problems with the program. If you're planning on attending part-time, you'll also want to ask how long it takes the average part-time student to complete the program and receive a degree. If the average student's stay seems excessively long to you, find out why; required courses could be offered seldomly, which may not fit into your schedule if you're a part-time student.

Type of Degrees Offered, including Joint Degrees

If you've done the self-analysis we recommended in the last chapter, you should know what general area you'd like to pursue in your business studies. But as you can see from the list of possible business degrees that we presented in Chapter 1, there are several degree options for each general area. If you want advanced studies in accounting, for example, you could pursue an M.B.A. with a concentration in accounting or an M.S. in accounting with or without a CPA certification *or* an M.Acc. Or you could get a dual M.B.A./M.Acc. If you're interested in both accounting and law, you could enroll in an M.S./J.D. degree program. Do you think you may want to continue on after your master's degree for a Ph.D., an M.D., or an Ed.D.? If you do, you'll need to look at schools that offer a doctoral degree in your field of interest as well, since you don't want to worry about transferring credits down the road.

In all likelihood, you'll probably find yourself choosing between an M.B.A. and an M.S. degree. You'll find many different opinions about which degree is better. If your background is in the liberal arts, for example, you may want to consider an M.B.A. over an M.S., since the M.B.A. will provide you with a general business curriculum as well as quantitative course work and an area of specialization. In all likelihood, an M.S. program will not provide you with as many general business courses as an M.B.A. program will. If you're in a quandary about which degree will be best for you, speak to those who are already employed in your field of interest. If they have M.S. degrees, do they wish they had received an M.B.A. degree instead, or vice versa? When you go on informational interviews, ask your contact about the value of both degrees. When they recruit, do they look only at those candidates with M.B.A. degrees? Along those lines, find out from each program which companies hire graduates with both M.S. and M.B.A. degrees.

> **In all likelihood, an M.S. program will not provide you with as many general business courses as an M.B.A. program will.**

Curriculum/Areas of Specialization

As we saw in the last chapter, it's important to think ahead to what you'd like to do in the future before you make the next step of applying to business schools. When you look at individual schools, be sure that the programs they offer are compatible with your career goals. If you're interested in investment banking, for example, be sure to apply to a school with a strong program and good reputation in that area. Having an M.B.A. will ensure that you've got the basic quantitative knowledge and business acumen that employers in the business world are looking for, but it may not be enough to help you land your dream job. To do that, it's important that you study at a well-regarded program that allows you to concentrate in a specific area of interest.

Check out what kinds of extra opportunities the programs you're interested in offer their students. These could include opportunities for study abroad, individual studies, honors programs, trips to off-campus seminars, guest lectures, and more. In other words, find out how the program supplements the classroom experience with out-of-classroom opportunities and extracurricular courses. Are program requirements rigidly defined, or is there some room for flexibility in choosing classes?

Another factor to consider when you're looking at a program's curriculum is its focus on business skills that will be applicable in the twenty-first century. Business analysts claim that the businessperson of the future will succeed based on his or her prowess in the areas of globalization, technology, and teamwork. How do the programs you're interested in incorporate these elements? Does the program have a forward-thinking curriculum that changes to keep up with the current trends in business, or have they been teaching the same courses for years?

Tuition, Fees, and Financial Aid

For many graduate students, cost is a determining factor in their decision of which graduate program to attend. Business school is no different. At some of the most expensive business schools, an advanced degree will cost more than $100,000 by the time all is said and done. Consider how big a factor cost plays in your analysis of schools. Think not only about the overall cost, but also about the return you'll get on your investment in a business school education. Given the starting salaries of those who receive degrees from the school versus cost of the school and the time it takes you to get your degree, how long will it take you to pay back the cost of your education? The GMAC suggests that you also factor in the income you may lose if you decide to enroll in studies full-time and the likelihood that you'll reenter the work force at a significantly higher salary. If you're enrolling part-time, they note, think about how much longer it will take until you get an advanced degree and start making the salary that goes with it. You may want to consider a more expensive school if its graduates make more money upon graduating than do graduates from less expensive schools. The more expensive schools are usually the ones with the most prestige in the field, so don't delete a school from your list purely because of its cost. In the long run, you may come out ahead financially with a degree from a more costly school.

When considering the cost of a program, keep in mind other factors that will affect the amount of money it will cost to get your degree. If you're moving to another location, what will your moving fees be? How much will you spend visiting friends and family back home? Look into the cost of living in the area to which you're moving. If rents are high, check out on-campus graduate dorms. If you won't be eating in the campus cafeterias, find out how expensive local grocery stores and restaurants are. Estimate the costs of books and supplies as well. All of this needs to be factored into the total cost of your education.

Unless the sky is the limit (or your employer is paying), you'll need to explore options for financing your business degree. We'll talk more about this in Chapter 5, but when you're gathering information about programs, pay particular attention to the grants, loans, scholarships, teaching or research assistantships, or work-study options that are available. Get data on how many business students receive aid each year and what the average aid package is. Keep in mind that federal financial aid is available only to students who attend eligible institutions. Make sure that the programs you're applying to have the proper accreditation if you'll be applying for federal aid. To find out if a particular college is an eligible institution, call the Federal Student Financial Aid Information Center at 800-4FED-AID (toll-free).

Faculty Reputation and Teaching Methodology

Another area you may want to consider when you're looking at business programs is the reputation of the program's faculty members. Studying

Keep in mind that federal financial aid is available only to students who attend eligible institutions. Make sure that the programs you're applying to have the proper accreditation if you'll be applying for federal aid.

with and learning from leaders in the field of business will look good to future employers and may help you build a network of contacts that will be invaluable to you in the future. Even more important than program faculty members' prestige is whether or not their areas of specialization match your areas of focus. Look at their backgrounds and publications. Do they coincide with what you want to learn? Finally, you may know from colleagues and friends that the professors in the business program at your local college are skilled motivators who bring out the best in each of their students and are accessible to their students at all times. Think about what kind of relationship you'd like to have with business school faculty members and whether or not the program encourages that kind of interaction.

Think too about your undergraduate experience. In what type of learning environment did you thrive? Maybe you went to a big school and didn't find large lecture halls with lots of students per class intimidating, or perhaps you graduated from a smaller school and are accustomed to a small, seminar-type learning environment that encourages class discussion. Different business programs will have different styles of teaching. Some programs use the traditional lecture approach, which is more structured; others use the case study method, which allows for more class participation. Some programs emphasize individual studies; others, group discussion and a team approach. Some programs may require a lot of writing; others may require that you do more presentations. Is the course work practical or theoretical-would you rather be sitting in a classroom discussing theories or solving a real-world business problem? Be sure to find out what teaching methodology the program practices to make sure it matches your learning style.

One piece of data that you'll need to look at when considering teaching methodology is the faculty-student ratio. Again, think about what makes you comfortable. If you have no problem with lecture classes where there are 50 or more students to 1 professor, by all means don't discount a program with a high student-teacher ratio. If you know that you'll learn best in an environment where you can get a lot of individual attention, be sure to find a program with a low student-teacher ratio. Find out from the school what this ratio is in the business school specifically, not just in graduate programs or campuswide. If they don't have an exact number on hand, talk to students who have gone through the program, or visit a few classes to see for yourself.

Facilities

As you're reviewing information about a school, pay particular attention to its on-campus facilities. The size of the main library is a good indicator of the quality of the school. You'll also want to ascertain whether the business program has its own library; such a perk could be invaluable to your studies. Make sure that the business library—or the main library, if there's no business library—keeps current on and has an extensive archive of national and international journals and periodicals that are relevant to the field in which you're interested. You don't want to have to search high and low for research materials when you're writing papers or preparing class presentations. Also, take note of the school's interlibrary loan program.

Find out all you can about each school's technical resources. If the school doesn't require that each student has a laptop upon enrolling, inquire whether their computer centers are capable of meeting student demand and about the quality of the equipment. If the business program doesn't have its own computer center, how convenient is the nearest one to your classes? Make sure that the centers have Internet and e-mail access as well as word-processing and spreadsheet software. These days, many classrooms are wired for Internet access, and many professors use the Internet to supplement lectures. Find out how far the business program has gotten along the information superhighway.

If you're planning on attending business school full-time and living on campus, gather information about graduate housing. As fun as it was to live in the dorms as an undergraduate—sharing rooms, lounges, bathrooms, and all the other amenities—you probably want to have more privacy as a graduate student. Are graduate students housed in dorms that are separate from undergraduates? Will you have your own room? Your own phone? Your own bathroom? Your own e-mail account? At some schools, graduate student dorms have a separate

Find out all you can about each school's technical resources. If the school doesn't require that each student has a laptop upon enrolling, inquire whether their computer centers are capable of meeting student demand and about the quality of the equipment.

library and cafeteria, and social events are planned for the students there. Be sure you know up front what your housing situation will be like before you enroll.

As a graduate student, you're undoubtedly going to need to blow off a little steam after a hard day's work in the classroom or the library. If pumping iron, shooting hoops, or running laps helps you do this, find out about the school's athletic facilities and graduate students' access to them. If relaxing and socializing are more your thing, get information about student lounges and snack bars across campus, particularly those that are part of the business school. You'll want to be sure that these facilities have hours that will be convenient to your schedule.

Services for International and Minority Students, Women, and Students with Learning Challenges

As we discussed in Chapter 1, more and more international, minority, and women students are enrolling in business school than ever before. Before you apply to a program, ask about the student body breakdown: What is the percentage of students enrolled from each of these groups? Beyond the numbers, find out what support you can expect to receive if you're a member of one of these groups. Does the university offer services for international, minority, and women students? Does the business program? Find out about the existence of student groups that can represent you, both campuswide and in the program specifically. Beyond that, look at the school's job placement rate data for international, minority, and women students: does the rate compare to that of its white, male students? Most importantly, try to speak to students who are currently enrolled in or have graduated from the program. Their insight on this subject will be invaluable.

Comparably, if you're a student with a learning challenge, you'll need to know whether the school and the program will provide you with the help that you'll need to succeed in your endeavors. Find out about note takers, extended test times, readers, or any other services you may have received as an undergraduate. You want to be sure that the program supports you as you work toward a degree.

Career Recruitment

What any business program can do for you in terms of your career is of paramount importance. In fact, many programs' reputations are based on the career success of their graduates. Find out how well each program that you're considering does in placing its graduates in good jobs. Most schools will have placement rate data available, but dig a little deeper. You want to know not only what percentage of students were placed and what their average starting salaries were but also *where* they were placed. Would you want to work for any of the companies on their list? If none of the students find jobs at Fortune 500 companies and you really want to work at a Fortune 500 company, by all means don't apply. You may also want to find out where graduates are several years down the road. You want to know whether the education they've received has helped them enjoy opportunities for advancement.

Along those lines, investigate the availability of internships while you're enrolled in the program. If you plan to attend full-time, check out whether the program can place you in a summer internship that closely matches your intended career upon graduating. Find out whether the internships are paid or unpaid.

Student Organizations/Services

Finally, you may want to investigate organizations and services for students around campus and in the business program. If you were involved in campus life as an undergraduate, make sure that you'll have those same opportunities for participation and leadership as a business school student. Get a list of the different graduate and business student organizations that you can join and see if any pique your interest. You probably won't have a lot of spare time on your hands as a graduate student, but if you want to get involved—and beef up your resume in the process—you should be able to do so.

Similarly, find out what the school and the program do to ensure each student's safety and health. If you're a part-time student, you'll probably be traveling to and from campus at night. Inquire about campus security, particularly in the parking lots around the business school and the library. Where can you go if you have a problem? Are the school's counseling centers available to business students? Does the

Find out how well each program that you're considering does in placing its graduates in good jobs.

business school itself have counselors to help you if you find the transition to advanced studies difficult? If you become ill, you'll need to access campus medical facilities. Find out about the services they offer and about their hours of operation.

CAMPUS VISITS

The best way to find out about a school or program is to visit the campus and see for yourself. How else will you be able to get the feel of the campus, see for yourself what the classroom experience is like, visit the library, and sample the cafeteria food? Remember, you'll be spending a significant amount of time here, so you want to be comfortable.

If you know it's just not the right place for you, you probably shouldn't enroll.

When to Visit

The best time to visit a campus is when classes are in session. Try not to go during homecoming week or parents' week, since the overall feel of the campus won't be the same during special events. Before you go, prepare a list of general questions that you'd like to ask admissions counselors, students, and professors. Make sure your list is the same for each school you plan to attend. This is your chance to find out what you can't discover from a school's literature or Web site, so be sure to ask all the questions you want.

What to Look for While You're on Campus

The best time to visit a campus is when classes are in session.

When you visit a campus, by all means take the student-run tour being offered by the admissions office. Listen closely to your guide. Does he or she sees enthusiastic about the school? Don't be afraid to ask your guide specific questions about his or her experience at the school.

When the tour is over, do some exploring of your own. Your first stop, of course, should be the business school. Look at bulletin boards in the business school office. Who is recruiting on campus? Any companies that you're interested in? How often are career events scheduled? Look for announcements for groups and clubs that you may be interested in joining and for social events planned by the school.

Gauge if the business school has the feel you're looking for, be it intense or friendly—above all else, you want to be comfortable here. If you can, grab a business school student and ask him or her about her experiences at the school. Have they been positive? Ask if you can sit in on a class that you may be taking if you enroll. Do the students look engaged, or are they dozing in their seats?

Next stop, the library and computer center. Do these facilities look up-to-date? Walk through the stacks in the library. You'll be spending a lot of time here. Are there enough tables for students to study? Is there a staff to help you? At the computer center, how many students are waiting for a PC? Check on the quality of the equipment, and inquire about the software packages installed on the machines. Be sure to make a note of the hours that the library and computer center are open.

If you'll be living on campus, check out the graduate student dorm. Ask if you can see a room and the bathrooms. Is there a cafeteria? Be sure to check it out. What kinds of amenities do you find in the dorm? Some graduate student dorms have their own libraries, lounges, vending machines, fitness rooms, and laundry facilities. You'll want to get a glimpse at them.

If you're looking at a school that's far from your home, go off campus and explore the environment around the school. Consider whether you'll want to go beyond the campus gates. Investigate restaurants, shops, clubs, museums, or anything else that's important to you.

> Let your intuition rule.

THE AFTERMATH

When you get home, let your impressions settle down for a while; you'll probably be experiencing some sensory overload. In the days ahead, follow up on any questions you may have thought of while exploring. Be sure to write thank-you notes to everyone who took the time to help you.

As you can see, there's a lot to think about when you're deciding to which business schools to apply. The best match for you is a choice that is subject to many considerations. Be sure to weigh carefully each of the factors that we've discussed in this chapter carefully to decide which are the most important to you. Only then will you be able to make the choice that's right for you.

Business School Information Worksheet
School Name:
Location:
Name/Phone Number/ E-mail Address of Business School Director:
Application Deadline:
Type of Program
Full-time?
Part-time (weekend, evening, summer, intensive)?
Distance?
Degrees awarded:
Amount of time needed to get degree?
Admissions Criteria
Minimum GMAT score required:
Minimum GPA required:
Is work experience necessary? How much?
Average number of applications yearly:
Percent of applications accepted:
Average GMAT score of entering students:
Average GPA of entering students:
Size
Size of school (total number of students):
Number of graduate students vs. number of undergraduate students:
Size of business program (total number of students):
Size of degree program (total number of students):

Setting and Environment
Campus setting (urban, suburban, rural):
Campus environment/business school environment (outgoing, relaxed, diverse, conservative, studious, etc.):
Curriculum
Core required courses:
Extracurriculars:
Areas of specialization:
Opportunities for study abroad:
Other learning experiences (trips, internships, etc.)
Faculty and Teaching
Faculty-student ratio in business programs:
Reputation of faculty:
Teaching methodology (lecture, case study, team projects, etc.):
Facilities
Library:
Technology on campus:
Athletics facilities:
Housing:
Student Services and Groups, Campuswide and in the Business School
Services for minority students:
Services for international students:
Services for students with learning differences:
Services for women students:
Business student groups and clubs:
Security:
Medical services:
Counseling:

Students	
Average age:	
Male-female ratio:	
Percentage full-time/part-time:	
Average years of work experience:	
Attrition rate:	
Career Placement in Business Program	
Internships available? Paid or unpaid?	
Career recruitment opportunities:	
Job placement rate data:	
Starting salaries of graduates:	
Companies at which students get jobs:	
Costs and Financial Aid	
Tuition:	
Room and board:	
Cost of living:	
Fees:	
Deposit:	
Financial aid available (work-study, grants, scholarships, loans, etc.):	
Amount of typical aid package:	
Percent of students receiving aid:	
Application Requirements/Date Sent:	
GMAT:	
Other tests:	
Transcripts:	
Recommendations:	
Essays:	
Application form:	
Application fee:	

The Application Process

So far, we've discussed the preparatory steps leading up to your decision to apply to business school. Now it's time to move on to the really hard part—submitting applications to the programs you've chosen. What, you thought it was all downhill from here? Far from it. How you prepare your business school application makes all the difference when it comes to getting accepted at your dream school. Read on to learn more about that special combination of timing, self-analysis, honesty, and accuracy that will have admissions officers clamoring to accept you into their programs.

TIMING AND DEADLINES

Most schools—and most business programs—have a filing period for applications of about six to eight months. During this time, the department accepts applications, reviews them, and offers attractive candidates a spot in their program. With such a large window, are you better off applying earlier or later in the cycle?

Most admissions counselors advise that, when it comes to filing your application, earlier is better. In their opinion, an early application has a better chance for admission for several reasons. Most importantly, submitting your application early shows that you are really interested in the program—a surefire way to impress admissions committees.

Although it may not necessarily be the case, if you wait until the last minute to send in your application, it may leave the impression that you see the program as a last resort. If you take it down to the wire, there's also a greater chance that your application will be prepared hastily, something any admissions committee worth its salt is sure to notice—and view negatively. Remember, these people are professionals; they've reviewed thousands of applications over the years, so they'll be sure to recognize it if you've rushed to complete the application.

Chapter 4

This will not reflect well on your candidacy. As we'll discuss later, the best applications are those that show readers that you have a well-thought-out plan for your future. A rushed application will make you look scattered—and not very serious about the program.

Other good reasons for applying early: At the beginning of the process, there are more spots available. Inevitably, the majority of candidates wait until later on in the admissions window to apply, so as the deadline nears, you'll be competing for the (fewer) remaining spots with a greater number of applicants. Also, at the beginning of the application process, admissions directors have no idea about whom will be applying to the program, so they're not very sure about how selective they can be about admissions. This could work in your favor, since early on, your application will be judged more on its own merit than on how it compares with others.

Most admissions counselors advise that, when it comes to filing your application, earler is better.

STAYING ORGANIZED

Different programs have different deadlines, so you'll need to stay organized throughout the application process. As you receive applications, you may want to file them in separate folders and note the program name and the deadline where you can see it easily. Be sure to note if the program has a rolling deadline, where applications are reviewed as they are received and spots are filled until the program is full, or a firm deadline, where your application must be submitted by a certain date.

GradAdvantage

GradAdvantage is a new application service developed by the Educational Testing Service and Peterson's. GradAdvantage can save you a lot of time and work by allowing you to apply on line to many graduate schools and M.B.A. programs. You enter your personal data, educational background, employment history, and activities only once, and this information is automatically posted to the application forms of the schools you select. You can then complete each application on line at your convenience, saving your work in progress whenever you've finished a session. You can write your essays using your own word processor and then upload them into your online applications. And you can submit the names of the people who will be writing your letters of recommendation.

GradAdvantage sends your application and your GRE, GMAT, and TOEFL scores (if applicable) via the Internet to the admissions office of the school you have designated. For more information, check the GradAdvantage Web site at www.gradadvantage.org.

TO HOW MANY SCHOOLS SHOULD YOU APPLY?

As you'll soon read, the business school application process can be fairly arduous, so you want to be sure that you apply to just the right number of schools. Too few and you may not be accepted to any; too many and you may go crazy filling out all those forms and writing all those essays! Make realistic choices. Look at the criteria of the schools in which you're interested and at your qualifications, and be honest with yourself. By all means, don't rule out your dream program if your GMAT is 10 points below their stated cutoff; but if your GMAT is 50 points below the cutoff, your GPA is a point below their cutoff, and you don't have any real work experience, you might want to save yourself the effort.

You may want to place the schools that you've chosen into three categories—reach schools, probable schools, and safety schools—and then go from there. Apply to a few reach schools (those that are longshots based on your academic record and other application materials), send more applications to probable schools (those to which you have a reasonable, realistic, and better-than-average chance of getting admitted), and send a few applications to your safety schools (those where you're sure you'll be accepted). Generally, safety schools won't be your first choices, but you may need to rely on them if you don't get accepted at your reach and probable schools. Don't, however, apply to any school that you wouldn't attend happily.

How you prepare your business school application makes all the difference when it comes to getting accepted at your dream school.

HOW DO BUSINESS SCHOOLS PICK STUDENTS?

When business schools review applications, they do not follow a magical formula, where GMAT + GPA + Work Experience + Personal Statement = Admissions. Most schools are looking to enroll an ideal community of students who will work well together in the program and benefit from the program's goals, so not just the straight-A students with high GMAT scores will be offered admission. Globalization in the field of business itself means that programs are looking for a more diverse student body that includes older students, women, minorities, international students, and students from small schools, big schools, Ivy League schools, and so on. This might all sound a little nebulous, but admissions directors want to enroll students that will be a good fit with their program, and every program has a different definition of what that good fit will be, based on a mix of professional, academic, and personal interests. If you've done your homework and are applying to those programs that you've determined will fulfill your career and personal goals, you're off to the right start. In other words, don't be discouraged from applying to a program that you feel is perfect for you just because your GMAT score falls slightly below their stated requirement. If all the other elements of your application show that you will be a valuable member of their team, your chances for admission will be favorable. By the same token, if you're an older applicant (more than 32 years old), you may feel that your chances for admission are lower because you do not represent the "typical" graduate student. On the contrary, in business school, older students are seen as offering professional experience, maturity, and real-world perspective—all highly valued in the business world.

So remember this when you're applying: at most schools, no single factor will count more than any other. As the old saying goes, "The whole is greater than the sum of its parts," and that's especially true in business school applications. Your tests scores, GPA, work experience, essays, and recommendations put together create a complete picture of your interests, strengths, and accolades. Weaknesses are overshadowed easily by strengths in other areas, so be sure to show off those strengths.

THE ELEMENTS OF AN APPLICATION

Form and Fee

Application forms can be downloaded from a school's Web site, obtained through the mail, or even, with services like GradAdvantage, submitted on line. When filling out your application, whatever form it takes, remember that accuracy and neatness count. If you must hand-write it (and you should try at all costs to avoid this), make sure that your handwriting is legible. If you type your application, check and double-check for typos, errors of alignment, and other potentially embarrassing gaffs. You don't want to start off on the wrong foot with the admissions committee. You may want to photocopy the blank form several times and fill out a few drafts before you complete the copy that you'll submit.

Before you send off the application, make a copy for your own records. Remember the fee. Ridiculous as it seems, every year admissions committees receive lovingly prepared applications—presented in beautiful folders or professionally bound—from well-meaning applicants who've forgotten to include the fee. No matter how well the rest of the application is prepared, this oversight simply doesn't look good.

> Applicants are evaluated as individuals. The environment in which they have studied or worked is relevant only when it is given meaning in the context of their life experiences.

Test Scores

Most business schools (but not all) require that prospective applicants submit scores from standardized tests, most often the GMAT, and the TOEFL, if you're an international student. When you take these tests, you'll be able to pick which schools you'd like your scores to be sent to; if you decide later on that you'd like your scores submitted to other schools, you'll need to make the proper arrangements to get them there.

Transcripts and Resume

You'll need to provide each program with a copy of your academic transcript from every school that you've attended. Don't forget to include transcripts from summer school programs, graduate work, or any classes you have taken since graduation. Allow at least a month to receive your transcript, and be ready to pay for each copy. Review your transcripts carefully to make sure that there are no mistakes, and remember to keep a copy for yourself.

Some programs will also ask you to include your resume or curriculum vitae (CV) as a summary of your work history. If you haven't updated your resume or CV lately, take the time to do so now. Include information about articles you have published or papers you have presented, volunteer work, and memberships and positions in professional societies. Have someone else review it for accuracy and spelling. Your resume or CV should highlight your accomplishments, responsibilities, and career progression, if applicable. If possible, show evidence of managerial and leadership skills while portraying yourself as a team player.

Letters of Recommendation

If you haven't updated your resume or CV lately, take the time to do so now.

Most business programs will require you to submit two or three letters of recommendation from your present employer or professors. If you're not comfortable asking these people, you can submit recommendations from a co-worker, a former boss, or someone else who can vouch for the quality of your work. When requesting recommendations, be sure to provide the recommendation writers with a summary of your accomplishments—perhaps your resume or academic transcripts—as well as some details about which programs you're applying to and the criteria by which you'll be judged. Supply them with labeled envelopes so they can seal the recommendations upon completing them. Give your recommendation writers plenty of time to write recommendations, as much as two or three months. Check in with them a month before the recommendations are due, and collect the recommendations from them yourselves; don't make them go to the trouble of mailing them for you.

Essays

By and large, all business programs ask candidates to respond to essay questions. The number varies from program to program; some ask candidates to provide just one personal statement that discusses their past and their goals, while others require candidates to respond to as many as five or more essay questions on separate topics. We'll walk you through essay questions in more depth later on in this chapter, but in general, admissions committees are looking for you to show them why you want to be admitted to their particular program, review your personal background and goals for the future, describe your accomplishments (and failures) and how they shaped you, and discuss activities that you enjoy outside of work and school.

Obviously, with some of these elements, you won't be able to exercise much control. The information you include on the form is basic general information about you—your stats, so to speak. Your transcripts and test scores, too, are what they are. You can't go back and change the grades you got in college (wouldn't it be great if we could do that?) or the scores you got on the GMAT (although you can take the test a few times, chances are that you won't improve you score that significantly with each try). How, then, can you show the admissions committees who you really are—the brilliant person behind the so-so GPA from that little-known college in rural Pennsylvania? With your recommendations and your essays, that's how. You have total control over these elements. By choosing the perfect people to toot your horn and by doing some tooting of your own, you can turn an average application into an outstanding one and swing those admissions committees in your favor.

> When choosing recommendation writers, look for people who can write well, who have praised you for being good at what you do, and who are enthusiastic about writing the recommendation. A bad recommendation can spell the end for your application.

WHAT YOUR APPLICATIONS SHOULD SHOW ABOUT YOU

Academic Profile

Business programs want to admit those who can survive the rigors of their program. For this reason, they look at your undergraduate GPA, which reflects classroom achievement, and your GMAT score, which is an indicator of your aptitude. As we've said before, however, having a high GPA and GMAT score don't necessarily guarantee admission, nor does a lower GPA or GMAT score take you out of the picture. When reviewing your transcript, admissions committees will look not only at your overall GPA but also at the progression of your grades and the kinds of courses you took as an undergraduate. Did you work hard to improve your grades after a slow start—or did you lose steam in your final years? Did you take advanced courses as electives—or did you fill you spare classes with easy introductory courses to beef up your GPA? Admissions committees will take note of this. They will also look to see if you've had any notable academic achievements or won any awards as an undergraduate or in the workplace. If this is the case, be sure that it's reflected on your application—if not in your transcripts, then in your essay, letters of recommendation, or resume.

Your undergraduate degree will have little effect on your chances for admission to most business schools, so don't think that your B.A. in English literature will be a hindrance. Remember that most M.B.A. programs offer or even require a core curriculum of basic business courses as part of the degree. However, you should, as we've discussed before, be able to show that you have general skills in economics, calculus, and statistics. If you didn't take these courses as an undergraduate, show on your application that you are planning to do so before being admitted to the program.

> **When reviewing your transcript, admissions committees will look not only at your overall GPA but also at the progression of your grades and the kinds of courses you took as an undergraduate.**

Personal Qualities

Admissions committees want to see that you are a clear-headed individual who has taken the time to think about your future and your goals. For that reason, make sure that your application is consistent throughout—in what you're trying to say about yourself and your plans for the future. You'll be judged less favorably if you don't show a clear purpose or if you jump from idea to idea.

Along those lines, your application is a direct reflection of your ability to communicate with others—think of it as a high-level sales pitch. Communication skills are essential for business leaders. As Brian Walker, Assistant Director of Admissions at Jesse H. Jones Graduate School of Management at Rice University in Houston, notes, "You can be smart and motivated and come up with the greatest strategies, but if you can't get them across to customers or to upper management, your ideas are worthless." Your application is your only chance to show admissions committees how well you can communicate; this makes the essays especially important.

Your application should show that you have the motivation and commitment to complete graduate work in business. Business programs are also looking for leaders who are capable of working as part of a team, so you'll need to show on your application that you have the right combination of initiative, ability to follow instructions, and capacity to work well with others.

Work Experience

The large majority of business programs want to see that you have a few years of solid work experience. According to Samuel T. Lundquist, Director of M.B.A. Admissions at the Wharton School of Business, "Career success is the most effective way to prove your potential for leadership in a managerial capacity." In business school, you'll be called upon to contribute to class discussions and projects in meaningful ways, and work experience will provide a context for your interpretation of what you'll learn in the classroom. When reviewing your application, business schools will want to see not only *where* you worked, but *what* you did while you were there. Did you move up? Did you take initiative? How did your contributions to the companies you worked for make you invaluable to them? Obviously, if you rose up over the years from the mail room to the board room, this will show admissions committees that you've got what it takes to succeed not only in business but also in their program—initiative, drive, energy, and dedication. Committees also want to know about your membership in professional organizations and your positions within these organizations and about research you've done in the field. All of this will paint a clear picture of you as a worker and, by extension, as a student.

Organization/Presentation

When you enter the world of business, you'll be called upon to present your ideas and the ideas of your company. How well you present yourself in your application will be an indication of how well you'll do

> **Business programs are also looking for leaders who are capable of working as part of a team, so you'll need to show on your application that you have the right combination of initiative, ability to follow instructions, and capacity to work well with others.**

at this task. Are you thorough? Did you supply the requested materials and the proper fee? Is everything spelled correctly? Check and double-check all the materials to make sure you haven't inadvertently sent the materials for another school. This is a huge mistake that will put a giant black mark on your application. Thoroughness and accuracy are key.

THE ESSAYS

We've included a special section on essays because business schools put a lot of stock in the quality of the essays that they receive from their applicants. Admissions committees count on essays to show them the real you, beyond the numbers and stats shown in the other elements of your application. In your essay, you show why you're serious about getting an advanced degree in business, exhibit what you can contribute to a particular program, and elaborate on what you've achieved on a personal, professional, and academic level. It's also the perfect opportunity to demonstrate that you are a clear thinker and that you can express yourself well. While essays are just a part of the overall admissions process, stellar essays can propel an otherwise average application into the "accept" pile, and poorly written essays may drop you to the bottom of the list.

Before You Begin

At every stage thus far—deciding whether business school is right for you, beginning the planning process, and picking schools—we asked you to take a good hard look at yourself. By now, you should have thought a lot about your motivations for wanting to go to business school and what you want to get out of it. Now is your chance to show the admissions committees that you've done some long, careful thinking about this. Even before you begin to write your essays, you should have a clear understanding of where you've been and where you're going. And not just in your professional life, either. How have your experiences—all of them, personal and professional—shaped you into the person that you are? And how does that relate to the course of study and profession you are choosing to pursue? This is what the admissions committees want to know. So before you begin writing your essays, take

> In crafting your application, your primary task is to stand out from other applicants with similar grades, test scores, work histories, and personal experiences.

stock of your background, your experiences, your abilities, and your goals. In each of these four areas, think about not just your professional experience but about your academic accomplishments and personal life as well. If you don't know how to begin, the following questions will get you thinking about where you've been and where you're going:

- What were my strongest subjects as an undergraduate? How did my academic experiences influence my choice of major and my decision to return to business school?
- When did my interest in the profession that I hope to enter after leaving business school first develop?
- What do I want to be doing in five years?
- What are my favorite extracurricular activities? Why do these mean so much to me?

Essay-Writing Tips

Give Yourself Plenty of Time

As soon as you receive each application, make note of the essay questions. How many are there? What questions are being asked? You want to be sure that you have plenty of time to thoughtfully answer each question before you return the application. The entire process of assessing the question, deciding on a structure for the essay and creating an outline, writing the first draft, and revising could literally take you months to accomplish. If you need to brush up on your writing skills, which admissions committees will be looking at, give yourself even more time.

Do Your Research

Before writing your essays, refresh your memory about the school and program. You don't want to regurgitate their pamphlet back to them, but you should show that you know your audience—in other words, what their program is all about. Don't go on about your dreams to pursue a career in the field of health-care management if the program doesn't offer course work in that area. This would make it look like you're applying to a completely different program! Look for key words

> Self-assessment helps you understand how your background led you to apply to business school—a must-have piece of information that will tell admissions committees why you want to and *should* attend their program.

in their literature that appeal to you. Do they stress teamwork, communication, or leadership? Why does this appeal to you, and what can you say about your history that would demonstrate this?

Follow the Directions

Whatever you do, don't let your essays run over the requested length. One of the things that admissions committees want to see is that you can respond to their questions in a concise way and that you follow the instructions that they've set out for you. You'll undoubtedly need to rewrite several times to hone down your answer to the acceptable length, but it's worth the effort. In your essay, get to the point quickly and then state your message succinctly. If you follow these guidelines, you'll have no problem meeting word limitations. If there's anything else that you feel you must say, incorporate it into another question or save it for your interview.

> The standing of your company in the business community, the variety of your work experiences, your advancement over the years, and your interpersonal skills in the workplace are just as important as your years of work experience.

Another sticking point with admissions committees: not answering the question that's been asked. Some applicants think that they can submit the same essay to several different programs, reasoning that the questions aren't all that different from program to program and that they can save themselves some time this way. Try to avoid this. If you look closely at the questions from program to program, you'll find that there will be many subtle and not-so-subtle differences. Unless each program that you're applying to is asking the standard "Why do you want a business degree?" question (and the likelihood of this is fairly rare), your essays should be tailor-made for the program to which you're applying. Admissions directors are often well aware of the questions that other programs are asking, so they'll recognize it if you're answering a question that's not their own.

Be Yourself

When responding to questions, be sure to take a stand that means something to you on a personal level. If you get bogged down in telling the committee what you think they want to hear and don't really believe in what you're saying, your essay will be less effective and will sound hollow. Across the board, admissions committees say that they "just know" when an applicant isn't being genuine. They've read enough essays to recognize those that do and don't ring true. Establish a personal connection to the question, and go from there. Don't worry about what you *should* be saying. Remember, there's no right answer. Your essays should distinguish you from the crowd and should show what's distinctive and important about you; only by answering the questions honestly can you do that.

Don't Make Excuses

Your essays can be an ideal place to address shortcomings in the rest of your application, but be sure that you do it the right way. Make your explanations short and to the point, and avoid sounding like a victim. Whatever you do, don't say, for example, "My professors in undergraduate school didn't like me; that's why my grades were so low." Take responsibilities for your failures, and show what you've learned from them. Don't overemphasize the negative; turn them into challenges that you've conquered and from which you've moved on.

Revise

Revising and re-revising will take your essays to a whole new level. Once you've written your first draft, step away for a while and then go back to it. Does the essay say what you really wanted to say? Read the essay for focus and purpose. Make sure that it answers the question being asked in a clear and concise manner. Will an outside reader be able to get to your point quickly and be persuaded by your argument? After you've reviewed your essay at this level, go deeper to the sentence level and look at every sentence carefully. Each sentence should follow smoothly from the one before it and should lead into the one following. Check to make sure that you've maintained a consistent voice throughout—you want to make sure it's you that's speaking, not the program's brochure or your undergraduate business professor. Make sure that your tone is appropriate for the circumstances. You want to sing your own praises without sounding boastful, and you don't want to be whiny. Finally, correct run-on sentences, grammatical errors, and passive constructions. Remember, how you tell your story is just as important as what the story says.

> Explain anything that could be construed as negative in your application. Do this as an addendum or in a cover letter, or ask one or more of your recommendation writers to address the issue in their letter.

Proofread, Proofread, Proofread!

We can't stress this enough—before you send out your application, you absolutely, positively must make sure that you haven't made any basic mistakes. A spelling error in the first line of an essay that describes how you're such a perfectionist is sabotage, plain and simple. Of course, you have a spell-checker built into your word-processing software, but under no circumstance should you depend on it to catch all the errors you may have made. In this case, you must resort to the tried-and-true methods used in days of yore (i.e., the days before computers). Print out your essays and read them forward and backward; challenge yourself to look for mistakes—rest assured, you'll find them. Read your essays several times, taking time between each reading. Ask someone who's a whiz at grammar and spelling to review your essays.

Use Outside Readers

A spelling error in your essay is sabotage, plain and simple.

Family, friends, colleagues, and professors will be invaluable assets as you write your application essays. Show them your essays (as well as the questions being asked), and ask for their honest opinion about the clarity and construction of the work. If the people closest to you can't understand what you're getting at, no admissions committee will be able to, either. Ask friends and family whether the essays show the real you, not just somebody who's read up on the program. Colleagues and supervisors at work will be able to tell you if you've stressed the right points about the field you want to pursue. Some applicants go so far as to hire professionals to help them write their essays. In general, admissions directors do not look highly on this practice. Remember what we said before about consistency? An essay that doesn't jive with the tone of the rest of your application is a dead give-away that you haven't written it yourself. Admissions committees are pros at picking out canned essays. Do the work yourself (with the help of those closest to you, not those who expect payment for the service), and your true voice will emerge. This is what admissions committees look for.

Answering Specific Types of Essay Questions

Questions about Your Career Goals

Almost every business program will ask you to evaluate your career thus far and discuss your career goals for the future. You should have no problem discussing what's already happened in the past and how this has affected you, but how can you clearly state what you want from your

What the Admissions Committee Wants to Learn from Your Essays

Who are you? This is your chance to tell them all about yourself—about your interests, your past, and your goals. In your essays, you should fill in the blanks of your application to provide a full-color portrait of yourself.

What can you bring to the program? Tell the committee why you're a great candidate for their program. Highlight the qualities that you possess that will benefit the program as well as your fellow students. Show them that you will be able to contribute to the school in a meaningful way.

Why do you want an advanced degree in business from this program in particular? Discuss those elements of the school's program that are appealing to you and the ways that they complement your goals. Of the hundreds and hundreds of programs offered, theirs was one of the most attractive. Be sure to tell them why you are interested in their program above all the others.

How have your experiences shaped you? Your life thus far has led you up to this point, and you've made the decision to apply to business school based on a variety of experiences that you've had and lessons that you've learned along the way. Describe the impact of these experiences and lessons—what you've gained, how you've changed, and what you've resolved because of them.

Where have your abilities taken you thus far? Where will they take you in the future? The approach here is twofold: First, you want to discuss those distinctive characteristics of yours that have helped you overcome adversity and have brought you success. Second, you want to describe how these same characteristics will help you not only succeed in the program but also contribute to your chosen field in the future.

future? Begin by basing your goals in the experiences that you've already had. This will give you a good jumping-off point. If you love what you do and want to take it a step further, begin by stating something like, "I've been interested in pursuing investment banking ever since I began my career as an assistant to a junior broker on Wall Street upon graduating from college." If you're not already in a business field but find that you're drawn to a certain aspect of business, you may want to describe how you came to this conclusion: "I knew after beginning my career as a computer programmer that it wasn't the job for me; it can be very solitary and isolating, and I enjoy working as part of a group. When I realized that my interest in technology could be parlayed into a career in information systems management, I knew that the next step would be to pursue a degree in business." The key here is to *personalize* your goals and make them more interesting to your readers. You may want to break down your goals into short-term and long-term goals to make them sound more thoughtful and realistic about where your degree will take you. Or you can identify certain areas of interest to you—strategy, marketing, or leadership—and how they could be translated into a future career.

> Two excellent approaches to organizing an essay: (1) Outline the points you want to cover, then expand them; or (2) jot down ideas as they come to you, then move them around until you create a logical sequence.

Questions about the Social You

Believe it or not, business school isn't just about learning the art of wheeling and dealing and then moving on to a high-paying job; it's also about spending time with people, about really getting to know your colleagues and professors, about creating a *community*. Business schools ask you to write essays about your extracurricular interests because they want to know whether or not you'll fit in and what you'll contribute to the community. Business school, and the world of business as a whole, for that matter, is a very social experience—you'll probably be asked to work in teams for presentations and group projects. Will you be able to get along with others in the group? Are you a participator? An initiator? More importantly, you need to show that you're a well-rounded person, someone who knows how to mediate that fine balance between work and play. You've got to show that you've got a "big picture" approach to the world. In today's job market, businesspeople need to be flexible. Show the admissions committee that you can roll with the punches.

Questions about the "Real" You

Questions like these usually manifest themselves in the form of: "Here's your chance to tell us something about yourself that we haven't asked yet." Be creative; after all, the school is giving you free rein to tell them what you want. Use this opportunity to tell them something that's truly unique about you, something that no other candidate can bring to the table. Relay an experience that really shaped your development or talk about someone you admire and why. If you decide to "let it all hang loose," however, stay within the guidelines of common sense. Don't talk about politics; don't talk about religion. Don't express any wildly out-of-the-norm viewpoints. Use humor if you wish, but only if you're comfortable doing so and if it's in good taste.

Questions about Your Ethics

After the scandals that rocked the business world in the 1980s, many business school programs began asking applicants about ethics. In asking questions about your perspective on ethics (e.g., "Relate an ethical problem you have faced and how you handled it"), business programs want to see that you are honorable, that you know the difference between right and wrong, and that you're not just going for a degree in business to make a quick buck. In short, you have to get across that you abide by a certain value system, both in your career and in your personal life. This can be a very sensitive subject for many; after all, at times ethics can be relative to the situation at hand. If you're asked a question about ethics, state your beliefs firmly. Waffling could show a susceptibility toward weakness, which will make you a less attractive candidate.

SAMPLE BUSINESS SCHOOL ADMISSIONS ESSAYS

On these pages we've printed for you a series of essays from a successful applicant to Columbia Business School in New York City. As you read these essays, think about the points we've raised in this chapter. What makes this candidate's essays stand out? Note how this candidate

Sample Business School Essay Topics

Describe the progression of your career to date. Why are you seeking a business degree at this point?

What are your career goals? How will an advanced degree in business help you achieve these goals?

Why do you want to obtain your degree from our particular program?

How has your background, experiences, and education influenced the person you are today?

In reviewing the last five years, describe one or two accomplishments in which you demonstrated leadership.

Discuss a nonacademic personal failure. In what way were you disappointed in yourself? What did you learn from the experience?

Discuss your involvement in a community or extracurricular organization. Include an explanation of how you became involved in the organization and how you help(ed) the organization meet its goals.

successfully makes his real-life experiences—in his career, in his personal life, and in his academic life—relevant to his desire to attend business school.

Question #1 asked the candidate to describe his career goals, how an M.B.A. would help his achieve these goals, and his reasons for applying to Columbia Business School (limit 1000 words).

The business world is full of many interesting opportunities and a vast array of sectors in which one can specialize. This financial world has global implications that are constantly changing, and therefore may leave a business leader feeling lost without a formulated plan of action. One needs to develop definitive paths and goals in order to remain focused. As a working member of the New York City financial world for the last three years, I have established certain goals that I am currently striving for as I journey on in my continuing career at Ernst & Young.

One such goal is the ability to manage people effectively and efficiently. I believe that in any line of work, the key to a successful business is how well that business is managed from a personal development perspective. Employees of any company must be given pertinent direction, sound training, and proper feedback from their managers to be more productive in their defined job roles and responsibilities. In order to provide employees with this development, job experience supplemented with a further academic education is extremely important. I feel that an M.B.A. will help me to attain this vital mix and provide me with the essentials of being a successful manager on the various engagements I encounter throughout my career at Ernst & Young.

A second career goal is to further expand my horizons and take a look at the whole picture. When I first began working in the "real world" as an auditor for Ernst & Young, I was placed on the Morgan Stanley engagement, which was one of the largest and most complex financial service engagements in our office. I was given job responsibilities that focused on such a small part of the ultimate goal. I was not privy to many of the other components that allowed my team to meet the client's demands and expectations. This was due to the fact that I lacked any prior experience in the financial service industry and that I was new to the engagement. As I continued on the engagement for the next three years, I was given more responsibilities and began to see more of the big picture. I began to develop a greater interest in financial services and wanted to see more aspects of the business. Thus far, I have been given the opportunity to see a vast array of areas at Morgan Stanley and at my current client, Lehman Brothers. These areas include front office trading operations on the fixed income and financing desks, middle office functions in fixed income cash and derivative instruments, back office operations on various trading desks, and multiple SEC filings. As I continue along in my career endeavors at Ernst & Young, I want to learn more about the financial industry and be able to look at the business from a much broader realm rather than the individual components for which I have been responsible. As I have much more to learn, I believe an M.B.A. will provide me with a window to see various new ideas and avenues from both a domestic as well as a global perspective. This will allow me to communicate more effectively to my clients and indicate to them specific inefficiencies in their business processes that I may be able to provide recommendations and assistance in improving.

Another goal is to continue developing my own experience and knowledge with the help of others. While experience in the work place is extremely important in attaining this goal, I believe it can only be enhanced in an academic arena where professors and other students can share their own work experiences with each other. This would provide me with different perspectives upon which I can look at my own experiences and current job responsibilities. Also, the ability to work with these people in an academic setting (e.g., through various class assignments that require group participation) would allow me to bounce my own ideas off others, while at the same time provide me with the opportunity to listen to what others have to say. The wealth of knowledge and personal resources available in the process of obtaining an M.B.A. is an endeavor I feel is too worthwhile to forgo.

The goals I have established above in furthering my career can be accomplished at most business schools. However, one of the distinguishing attributes of obtaining my M.B.A. at Columbia University is the New York element. As mentioned previously, for the last three years I have been working as an auditor for Ernst & Young in New York City, primarily on financial service companies, including Morgan Stanley Group and Lehman Brothers, both highly reputable and profitable companies centralized in New York. The experience I have received from working on these engagements has made me realize the advantage of being in New York, as I truly believe I would not have obtained as unique an experience anywhere else. Columbia, itself a highly reputable and professional business school, has that same advantage, which would allow me to strengthen the New York business experience while at the same time bring people from many different business backgrounds to the New York arena. The contacts I would make at Columbia, from the versatile faculty to my educated peers, would help me develop into a more knowledgeable member of the domestic and global business communities.

Question #2 asked the applicant to describe an accomplishment in which he demonstrated leadership (limit 500 words).

When I was a senior in high school, I decided to try something unique. As a music aficionado for many years with piano lessons and countless 45s, I decided to try out for the spring musical *Grease*. I had never sung before, but decided to give it a try. Even though this was not Broadway, I was still in shock when I was given a part in the show and had to sing. The show went surprisingly well, and I decided that I wanted to continue my singing endeavors as a hobby when I went to college the following year.

I attended Boston College in the fall of the following year. I discovered a group called the Boston College Chorale, which was a highly talented choral group of approximately 150 men and women. The big attraction to the group was that it traveled abroad for a week in the spring to perform, which included Italy, where the group attended a papal audience to sing. I found this intriguing, and I decided to try out during my first semester. I was accepted into the group and met many diverse and interesting people during my first year.

In my second year, I became more and more involved with the group. An interesting facet of the group was that it was led by students. There were eight officers, comprised of college juniors and seniors, who had various group responsibilities. Toward the end of my second year in the group, the annual elections for new officers was held. Because of my increased interest in and commitment to the group, I decided to run and became one of four officers elected. The officer positions were two-year commitments, and each year the officers would vote on new titles for each officer.

At the end of my first year as an officer, the internal elections for the officer titles were held again. I was voted president of the group for my senior year. I knew this role would be quite challenging and time consuming, but I accepted it gladly and was ready to face the numerous responsibilities for the upcoming year.

I had to make various decisions for the group with the efforts of the other officers. I was ultimately responsible for ensuring that the concerts were planned and advertised in a timely manner, the university funding provided to our group was properly utilized, the annual trip abroad was in order from the accommodations to the performances, and the social events were organized. I felt the year went smoothly and that the group of officers worked well together. I was able to demonstrate my leadership role to the best of my abilities. Members of the group showed their appreciation to me and to the other officers at the end of the year. I had an overwhelming sense of accomplishment at the end of the year as I graduated from Boston College, ready to face further challenges that would require my leadership abilities.

Question #3 asked the applicant to discuss a nonacademic personal failure, describing how he was disappointed in himself and what he learned from the experience (limit 500 words).

About a year and a half ago, my then-fiancée and I were returning from my college roommate's wedding in Rhode Island. It had been a long day for us, and we were taking turns driving back to New Jersey. When we got to New York, I told my fiancée that I would drive the rest of the way home to give her a chance to rest.

As I began my part of the drive, I was attempting to make a left-hand turn to get back on the highway. I did not see the car coming from the opposite direction until I had already started to make the turn, and our car was struck on the passenger's side. The sound was chilling. My fiancée's window had completely shattered, and I noticed that there was blood on her forehead. She said she was alright, except that her lower body was in pain. Medical help seemed to come instantaneously. The paramedics slowly removed her from the vehicle, and she was sent to the nearest hospital.

The whole experience put me in shock. I had this horrid sense of guilt and failure. I felt I had let her down tremendously with my mistake. After the doctors examined her, the final diagnosis was that she needed a few stitches on her forehead and that she had fractured her pelvis, which would require several weeks of bed rest until it healed on its own. She was going to be fine, which relieved me. The feelings of remorse, however, were still overwhelming. I sat down by her side after the doctors had left for the night and looked into her eyes and told her that I was so sorry for doing this to her. She grabbed me and told me that there was no reason to apologize. This was an accident, and the experience made her realize that she could not wait to spend the rest of her life with someone who cared so much for her.

I was in disbelief. How could she stay so calm after all I had done to her? I did not understand why she was not more angry with me. Over the next few months the scenes from the accident would play over and over again in my head. "If only" would be said in my thoughts repeatedly. I was angry with myself, and I felt that I was incapable of protecting my future wife.

My fiancée recovered fully, and we continued with our wedding plans for the next summer. I began to realize that since the accident, our faith in one another strengthened. The bond between us dispelled any doubts in the trust we had for one another. My feelings of guilt began to dissipate. When I realized how much she trusted me after the accident, I knew that any feelings of failure I would have in the future would be comforted with this trust.

Question #4 asked the applicant to discuss his involvement in a community or extracurricular organization, including an explanation of how he became involved in the organization and how he helped the organization meet its goals (limit 250 words).

I am currently involved in a community service organization sponsored by my company, Ernst & Young, called the "One-To-One Mentoring Program." I learned about the organization from other people at E&Y involved in the program. The goal of the program is to develop a relationship between a member of the Ernst & Young community and a high school student from the Bronx.

These students do not have much direction, nor do they have an abundance of opportunities. Many of them come from single-family homes with very little money. The program is voluntary on their end as well as ours, which makes the relationship one of choice from the very beginning. As present members of the working community, we are to share our experiences with the students and try to motivate them to continue on in their education. In addition, we are to be a friend who will listen to any of their problems or concern.

My current mentee is a sophomore who is bright but lacks motivation. I try to stress to him the importance of doing other activities after school, where he can make new friends and strive for additional goals. I also explain to him how important it is to complete his education. I use my own experiences in high school to help make him realize the importance of achieving goals. His grades have begun to improve, and he has started to look for part-time employment after school. In this respect I believe I have helped in meeting certain goals of the organization as our mentor/mentee relationship continues to strengthen.

INTERVIEWS

Many schools require that you interview with admissions committees and faculty members before you are admitted to the program. If you're asked for an interview, you should be glad, since chances are that you've made it to the program's short list of candidates. Even if the program doesn't require it, going on an interview is another great way to take some initiative and swing the vote in your favor.

While interviewing, don't simply rehash your resume and transcripts. This is the perfect chance to tell the admissions committee something they *don't* know about you from your application. Before you go on the interview, think about the questions that you might be asked and how you'll answer them, especially the biggie: "Why do you want to go to school *here*?" Think about those things that you want the interviewer to remember about you. However, try not to prepare speeches, as this won't sound natural when you're sitting face-to-face with the interviewer. The interviewer wants to see that you'll fit into the program, so be yourself. You'll be more natural and appealing if you don't try to put on an act.

Show the interviewer that you're well-versed about their program, and describe what you plan to contribute to it. Bring a copy of your resume or CV, your application (especially your essays), and any examples of your work that you feel are important. Don't ask about

> Even in a casual interview, certain topics are *always* off limits: profanity, tasteless jokes, sex, and your love life. And please don't talk about mom and dad—remember, you're in the adult world now.

financial aid; the interview is not the time to discuss these details. Be proactive—think of some questions that you'd like the interviewer to answer. Finally, dress professionally and be on time. The simplest rules are usually the most important. After you leave, be sure to write a thank-you note to the interviewer.

Tough Interview Questions

Why an M.B.A. now?

Tell me why you think our program is the one that's right for you.

Describe some examples of how you've demonstrated leadership.

What are your career aspirations?

What do you do to relax?

Give three words that best describe you.

Why did you choose your undergraduate major? Do you regret it?

Describe instances where you've worked as a member of a team to get a job done.

What is your definition of success?

Describe someone who's been an inspiration to you.

Where do you see yourself five years from now? ten years from now?

What do you find most frustrating about your present job?

Tell me about your biggest failure and how you rebounded from it.

What will you do if you're not accepted to this program?

So, tell me a little more about yourself . . .

DECIDING WHICH SCHOOL IS RIGHT FOR YOU

You've waged the battle, and the offers for admission are piling in. Now it's time for you to decide which program you'll attend. Faced with any number of attractive choices, this will be a daunting task. First, try to separate the hype from the reality. The programs that accept you will likely be barraging you with phone calls, letters, and e-mails from admissions counselors, students, and faculty members. When they call, ask the questions that you've been dying to ask but were afraid to in your interview. Now that they want you, the ball is in your court. Review the strategies that you used in the last chapter that helped you pick schools. Of the schools at which you've been accepted, which meet the criteria you originally found most important? Have your criteria changed at all through the admissions process? Revisit each campus at which you've been accepted, and really take a good look around. Attend special on-campus events that you've been invited to, and pick the brains of those in attendance. What do they like about the school? Why do they think you'd be a good match there? In the next chapter, we'll look at sources of financial aid for business school students. Be sure to find out *all* the details about the costs of the program—and about any available sources of aid to help you pay for it—before you sign on the dotted line. Resist making a hasty decision; be sure that you've weighed all the facts before you make your final choice.

Paying for Business School

Going to business school is a big investment—of your time, your energy, and especially your money. You'll undoubtedly have to depend on a variety of sources to pay for business school—loans, scholarships, work-study, even money from your family (if they're willing). As always, good preparation will ensure that you get the money you need and won't go broke paying it back.

Before you sign on the dotted line at any school, be sure you are well-informed about *all* the costs entailed in attending. As we'll discuss later, when budgeting for business school, you have to take into account not only the tuition charged by the program, but also any fees the school charges, the cost of living in the area where you'll be attending the program, and a vast assortment of extras, including insurance and medical expenses, transportation, and entertainment. Unless money is no object, the total cost of attending should be one of the most important criteria you consider when looking at schools.

Some students find that it's worth their while to spend big bucks to attend the most selective programs; others don't. When looking at a program and its costs, calculate how rapidly you'll get a return on your investment. As we discussed in Chapter 3, find out what the starting salary is for students graduating from the program, and then look at all the costs of attending. Is it worth it? Will you recoup the money that you've spent on the program in no time, or will you spend years paying back the loans that you had to incur to get through?

WHERE AND WHEN TO BEGIN

You should start exploring sources of financial aid as soon as you begin thinking about business school. When gathering information about specific schools, *always* request information about aid. After you've narrowed down your choices of programs to those to which you'd like to apply, contact their financial aid offices and schedule an appointment to speak with a school aid officer. Investigate each and every source of aid that the school and the program offer; some schools have specific financial assistance schemes that include grants, scholarships, work-study, and loans. Find out about school- and program-specific aid before you begin looking at outside sources. File all applications for aid that the school and program require *on time*.

Many outside resources are available to help you seek out the best sources of aid. Peterson's *Grants for Graduate & Postdoctoral Study* is a listing of more than 1,400 fellowships, grants, and internships that you can search by field of study; the volume also provides advice about how to apply for and win these sought-after awards. Appendix 2 at the back of this book lists other print resources that you may find helpful. Remember, this list is by no means exhaustive. We encourage you to go to your local bookstore, to your company's human resources office, or to your local library to seek out other books on aid. A vast amount of materials is available to help you.

The Internet is also an excellent source of information about financial aid. Begin with the Web sites of the schools to which you're applying. From there, you can search for information on private loans, government loans and grants, scholarships, internships, and much more. Appendix 2 will get you started with a list of financial aid–related Web sites. You can download applications for aid from most private lenders' Web sites or submit requests for aid to them directly on line. A word of caution, though: Beware of any site that asks you to send them a fee to process a request for any type of aid, especially scholarships. Before you send money or give your credit card number to *any* organization, do a little investigating to find out if the organization is reputable.

If you wisely go about your search for financial aid, you shouldn't have to pay money to get money.

TIMING, DEADLINES, AND APPLYING FOR AID

The first step in the financial aid process is to complete and submit all of the required applications. Procedures vary from school to school, so above all else, make sure that you check with the financial aid office at

> According to the Graduate Management Admissions Council, the yearly cost of a M.B.A. program can range from less than $5,000 to more than $70,000 for tuition, living expenses, books, and travel to and from the program.

each program about specific deadlines and guidelines. In all likelihood, you will have to complete the Free Application for Federal Student Aid (FAFSA). This form is required for all students who wish to receive federal and state financial aid; even if you're not applying for federal aid, most programs will have you fill out the form anyway, as it provides them with the information that they'll need to process any aid request. You can pick up a copy of the FAFSA from the program's financial aid office or fill it out on the Department of Education's Web site at www.fafsa.ed.gov.

The program may also require you to complete additional school-specific applications to determine whether you're eligible for funds from the institution. Remember, some of the best sources of aid that you may find will be from the schools and programs themselves, so be sure to fill in all the information requested and to submit the forms by the deadlines. When it comes to financial aid, deadlines are crucial; practically every student applies for financial aid, so you don't want to be disqualified because you didn't hand in your forms on time.

Getting aid isn't always quick, and it's certainly not easy. You'll spend a lot of time filling out forms and stressing over deadlines, so the more prepared you are when you begin, the better off you'll be. Determine what is needed for each aid application as soon as you can, and figure out the best way to remind yourself of deadlines. Sometimes, you'll need to show a certain GPA or financial need or will need to submit essays or letters of recommendation. Make several copies of all supporting materials at the beginning of application process and keep them handy.

Once your forms are received and reviewed by the schools' financial aid offices, your eligibility for assistance is determined. You are then sent an award notice informing you of the assistance that you are eligible to receive, both from the government and from the school. Make sure that you respond to the award letter as instructed by the school. If you are instructed or advised to apply for loans, be sure to complete those applications, sign any promissory notes, and return your application to the lender.

> Apply for financial aid even if you don't think that you'll need it. You never know what will come up over the course of your studies, so be sure that you're prepared.

WHO OFFERS AID?

Institutional Resources

Some schools offer institutional loan programs to help you with educational expenses. The financial aid administrator can tell you what you'll need to do to apply for a loan from the school. Your school may also offer a variety of scholarships and grants that could be awarded based on either need or merit. Many graduate students use teaching

Questions to Ask Before You Apply for Financial Aid

- What is the purpose of financial aid, and what do I need to know about the process?
- What should I be doing now to prepare for meeting the cost of my education?
- What eligibility requirements must I meet to obtain financing for my degree?
- What options/programs are available to me at the schools I'm considering?
- How do I apply for financial assistance, and what forms are needed?
- When should I apply for financial assistance?
- Will my parents be expected to provide any of their financial information?
- What is done with the information I provide?
- What should I know about the assistance I am offered, including grants, loans, work study? What will be expected of me to maintain such aid?
- What can I do to reduce the amount I have to borrow?
- What options will I have for working while I obtain my degree?
- What impact will the money I borrow have on me after I get my degree?

assistantships to pay for the cost of their education. A typical teaching assistantship requires a commitment of about 20 hours per week. You might also want to check with your school to see if they offer other on-campus employment opportunities that are not based on need or merit. Explore internship opportunities that are available at the school; a paid internship enables you to receive financial support while gaining work experience and, in some cases, academic credit.

Federal and State Financial Aid

The U.S. Department of Education provides financial assistance for students who attend eligible institutions. To determine your eligibility for these programs, you must complete the financial aid process established by the schools to which you're applying as well as that of the federal government. Aid programs that are offered by the federal government include Federal Subsidized Stafford Loans, Federal Unsubsidized Stafford Loans, Federal Perkins Loans, Federal Pell Grants, Federal Supplemental Educational Opportunity Grants, and Federal Work-Study Programs. Most state governments also offer grants, loans, and scholarships to their residents. Each state has a different FAFSA submission deadline, so be sure to keep this in mind when you're applying for aid. For a list of contacts that can answer questions about aid available to residents of your state, consult Appendix A at the end of this chapter.

When applying for aid, keep these pointers in mind:

- Complete every single form, and do it neatly.
- Read all of the instructions carefully before you begin.
- Answer all of the questions completely; do not leave any questions blank.
- Consistency is important when answering questions; if your forms raise any red flags, aid awards may be delayed.
- Apply early, or at least by the deadline.
- Keep copies of all of the forms you submit.

Private and Alternative Financing

Foundations, corporate sponsors, and individuals offer millions of dollars of aid every year through scholarships, grants, internships, and loans either directly to you or to you school, which then administers the awards. Private sponsors establish their own application procedures and eligibility criteria. You may need to do a little work to uncover all of the private aid that you're eligible to receive and to shop around for the loans that offer the best interest rates and terms of repayment—but the work you put into this process will be well worth the effort. To begin your search for private sources of aid, consult Appendix B at the end of this chapter and the print and Web resources listed in Appendix 2 at the end of this book.

Other Financing Options

Check with the schools you're interested in to see if they offer payment arrangements to lessen out-of-pocket expenses. At some schools, you can divide tuition and other fees out over the course of a year rather than having to pay everything up front. Several private organizations also offer tuition payment plans; these include Academic Management Services (800-635-0120, toll-free), Advantage School Tuition Payment Program (503-636-7175), FACTS Tuition Management System (800-624-7092, toll free), Key Education Resources Monthly Payment Plan (800-KEY-LEND, toll-free), and USA Group (800-348-4605, toll-free). If you have a steady source of income, such an alternative could be a godsend.

If you work while attending school, your employer may provide tuition assistance as a benefit to you, so be sure to ask if you qualify for this assistance and what you must do to maintain your eligibility. In most cases, you'll need to pay for your classes up front and then be refunded upon successful completion of your course work ("successful" is usually defined by maintaining a certain grade point average, usually a B average or better). Every company has its own rules, however, so be sure to find out all the details before you apply to receive aid or to enroll in a program. If your company doesn't offer this benefit, you may want to make a persuasive argument to your boss for doing so; with the present boom in the economy, employers are always looking for ways to keep good employees, and tuition reimbursement is a great way to do this. Be sure that you are aware of the tax ramifications of accepting tuition reimbursement from your employer. In some cases, these funds may be taxed as income.

If you are a veteran and have completed at least one year of active service, Veterans Educational Benefits are available for graduate study. The amount of the benefit for which you are available depends on your length of military service, the number of dependents you have, and how many course credits you are carrying. For more information, check with the veterans' affairs offices at the schools to which you're applying or call the Veterans Affairs Department at 202-233-4000.

These creative means of financing your graduate education are just the beginning. If you look hard enough, you'll find vast resources to which you can turn to pay for business school. Before you take out a loan, put in the time to investigate every source of aid for which you may be eligible. Chances are that you will end up borrowing at least some of the money that you'll need to pay for business school, but you want to keep this amount as low as possible.

Don't waste your money on fee-based scholarship matching services. All the information that you'll need can be found on the Web and in various print resources.

THE DREAM: SCHOLARSHIPS

The most prized form of financial aid is, of course, the scholarship. Hundreds of thousands of scholarships and fellowships are available every year. Most are reserved for students with special qualifications, like academic talent. But awards are also available to students who are interested in a particular field of study, to those from underrepresented groups, or to students who demonstrate financial need. Scholarships are offered by the schools themselves and by private organizations or individuals. The trick, of course, is to find out about the scholarships that may be available to you. There are several free scholarship databases available on line—*free* is the operative word here. Don't waste your money on fee-based scholarship matching services. All the information that you'll need can be found on the Web and in various print resources. Log on to as many scholarship search sites as you want, and compile information on scholarships that you're interested in. Then submit away! The good thing about scholarships is that there's no limit to how many you can get.

Myths about Scholarships

There are many widely held myths and misconceptions about scholarships. Perhaps it's because of the many different kinds of scholarships available or the variety of requirements needed to get them. Maybe it's because the process is time consuming and sometimes complicated. Whatever the reason, several scholarships myths are out there, so we'd like to take this opportunity to dispel some of them.

Myth #1: Billions of scholarship dollars go unclaimed. Most universities will tell you that they seldom have unawarded scholarships, and, if they do, it's usually because of timing or because of the highly restricted nature of a small number of scholarships. The "billions of dollars" figure comes from unused employee tuition benefits, which account for about 85 percent of unclaimed aid dollars. The number of unused scholarships is actually miniscule.

Myth #2: I can't possibly get a scholarship with all the competition out there. Alan Deutschman, author of *Winning Money for College*, received a degree from Princeton University for practically nothing by taking the initiative to enter scholarship contests wherever and whenever he could find them. As Deutschman claims, there are a lot of contests out there; you just need a little resourcefulness to seek them out. Not all scholarships are for A students; some are for those with a particular interest, those from a particular ethnic background, those affiliated with professional and fraternal groups, and so on—the list is endless. Another tactic is to look locally for opportunities in churches, civic organizations, and other groups. You won't believe the number of opportunities that you'll find if you just look hard enough.

Myth #3: Scholarship searches are worth paying for. As a prospective student, you have a wealth of information at your fingertips. For starters, visit your library, search the Web, and browse through bookstores—you'll soon find that you don't need to pay anybody for what you can do for free.

Myth #4: I'm a top student, so I don't have to seek out scholarships. They'll come to me. Don't take it for granted that you'll get a free ride through business school. The odds are not in your favor. Very few students are lucky enough to get through college on scholarships alone—and in graduate school, it's practically impossible. Therefore, we strongly encourage you to explore all the options that are available to you for funding your business degree, including loans, employer-funded tuition remission, and work-study.

Scholarship Scams

Unfortunately, there are a lot disreputable people who make a killing by taking advantage of students searching for aid. The Federal Trade Commission (FTC) claims that several unscrupulous companies promise you scholarships, grants, or fantastic aid packages; many use high-pressure sales pitches at seminars where you're asked to pay them immediately or risk losing out on the "opportunity." According to the FTC, several legitimate companies can get you access to lists of scholarships for a fee or compare your profile with a database of scholarship opportunities and provide a list of awards for which you may qualify. The difference? Legitimate companies never promise or guarantee scholarships or grants. The FTC (www.ftc.gov) advises you to keep your eyes open for these tell-tale claims:

> If you attend a seminar on scholarships, be wary of "success stories" or testimonials of extraordinary success. Instead, says the FTC, ask for a list of at least three local families who have used the company's services in the last year.

- "The scholarship is guaranteed or your money back." No one can guarantee that they'll get you a grant or scholarship. Refund guarantees often have conditions or strings attached. Get refund policies in writing—before you pay.
- "You can't get this information anywhere else." There are many free lists of scholarships. Check with your school, your employer, or your library before you pay someone to do the work for you.
- "May I have your credit card or bank account number to hold this scholarship?" Don't ever give out your credit card or account number on the phone without getting information in writing first. This may be a set-up for an unauthorized withdrawal.
- "We'll do all the work for you." Don't be fooled. You must apply for scholarships or grants yourself. There's no way around it.
- "The scholarship will cost some money." Don't pay anyone who claims to be "holding" a scholarship or grant for you. Free money shouldn't cost a thing.

- "You've been selected by a 'national foundation' to receive a scholarship," or "You're a finalist" in a contest that you never entered. Before you send money to apply for that scholarship, check it out. Make sure the foundation or program is legitimate.

If you're approached by someone who you think is a scam artist, contact the FTC's Consumer Response Center at 877-FTC-HELP (toll-free).

Before you take out a loan, put in the time to investigate every source of aid for which you may be eligible.

THE REALITY: LOANS

We're not trying to discourage you from going out and seeking a scholarship (or a dozen scholarships, for that matter), but the reality is that you'll probably need to take out a loan to pay for part of your business degree. There are fewer scholarships and grants at the graduate level, unfortunately, and competition for assistantships and internships can be tough; there simply isn't enough money to go around for everyone. But never fear—scores of low-interest loans are available to help you make ends meet.

Student Loans from the Federal Government

Federal education loan programs offer lower interest rates and more flexible repayment plans than most private loans; they also do not require credit checks or collateral, as most private loans do. Federal loans can be either subsidized, where the government pays the interest while you're in school, or unsubsidized, where you pay all the interest (these payments can be deferred until after you graduate). To receive a subsidized Stafford Loan, you must be able to demonstrate financial need. All students, regardless of need, are eligible for unsubsidized Stafford Loans. With Stafford Loans, graduate students can borrow $18,500 per year; of that, $8,500 is subsidized. Many students combine subsidized loans with unsubsidized loans to borrow the maximum amount permitted each year. Perkins Loans are awarded to students with exceptional financial need. With this program, the school acts as the lender, using a limited pool of funds provided by the federal government. The amount of the Perkins Loan that you'll receive is determined by the financial aid office; the limit for graduate students is

$5,000 per year, with a cumulative limit of $30,000 for undergraduate and graduate loans combined. (Some institutions participate in the Expanded Lending Option program, wherein they can offer higher loan limits for Perkins Loans.)

Student Loans from Private Institutions

Many students must turn to private loans after they have tapped into all other sources of aid. Fortunately, several low-interest student loans are available through many lenders. (See Appendix B at the end of the chapter for a select listing of loans that are meant specifically for graduate students and business students.) If you're a wise consumer, you'll shop around for a loan that will offer you the best interest rate and terms of repayment. Remember, you should be certain that you have exhausted all other options for paying for your education before you consider a loan. You may not want to approach your parents for money, but chances are that their interest rates are more lenient than any that you'll find at the bank! They may have even saved some money for you in the hopes that you'd go back to graduate school some day. It can't hurt to ask.

Selecting the Best Private Loan

According to Access Group (www.accessgroup.org/students/financing/comparing.htm), you should find out the following information about each of the loans that you are being offered before you actually apply for a loan: loan amount being offered and maximum loan eligibility, cosigner options and requirements (if any), interest rate, impact of your credit history on loan approval, repayment terms and grace periods, deferment terms and forbearance options, the reputation of the lender, and any value-added features of the loan.

The school certifies the amount that you are eligible to borrow; note whether this amount is the annual maximum allowed under the loan program or if you can apply for more funds if you need more assistance later in the year. Be sure to check if the program has an aggregate maximum, or maximum total amount of debt allowed under the program; keep track of how close to the maximum you are. Some state, institutional, and private loan programs require that you obtain a

> The federal government is the largest single source of student aid, with more than half of all students in American higher education receiving some kind of federal assistance. The GMAC reports that practically all federal aid to management students is in the form of student loans.

Some state, institutional, and private loan programs require that you obtain a creditworthy cosigner to apply for their loans; in some cases, applying with a cosigner may reduce the cost of the loan.

creditworthy cosigner to apply for their loans; in some cases, applying with a cosigner may reduce the cost of the loan.

Note when the interest starts accruing on the loan and find out whether the interest rate is fixed—set for the life of the loan—or variable—tied to an index that may change periodically. If it's variable, check how the rate is calculated, how frequently it's adjusted, and whether or not it has an upper limit. You should also know when the interest is capitalized, that is, when the interest is added to the principle of the loan. As we've already mentioned, a credit check is not required to apply for a federal student loan. However, private lenders will undoubtedly run a credit check on you. If you have credit problems, you may have trouble getting a loan. We'll talk more about your credit rating later on in this section.

Access Group advises that you review the number of years that you will have to repay each loan and the amount of time that you have between graduation and the start of repayment (i.e., the grace period). The longer your repayment and grace periods, the more interest you'll be paying. However, some borrowers find it necessary to have longer repayment periods to keep monthly costs lower. Also, apprise yourself of the loans' forbearance and deferment options in the event that you need to postpone repaying them. Most education loans offer deferments to those who return to school or are completing an internship or residency that is needed for obtaining a degree or license.

The reputation of the lender is of the utmost importance. You may want to check the lender's track record with making loans to students. Do they specialize in student loans, or is this only a small part of their business? Before you borrow from any private institution, ask financial aid administrators about the lenders that you're considering; you may also want to ask fellow students about their experiences with various lenders. You want the application, contact, and tracking processes to be as convenient as possible, so check with your lender about value-added features, like online services and toll-free customer service lines. With the best programs, these are available 24 hours a day, 7 days a week. Access Group offers graduated repayment options, which allow for lower payments during the first few years after graduation; payment amounts increase later when borrowers are more established in their careers. Check all your options before you apply; remember, the lenders want your business, so they should be able to accommodate your needs.

Loans and Your Credit

To get a private education loan, you must demonstrate a good credit history. The lender requests a copy of your credit profile and your credit score from an authorized reporting agency; then they review these records to ascertain your creditworthiness, which is based on your past credit performance. Your credit history is maintained by an authorized credit reporting agency and is sent to potential creditors when requested. If you have at least one credit card, a car loan, undergraduate student loans, or any other type of personal credit, you've got a credit history. A credit report includes information about the types of debts you have, the current balances of these debts, your payment performance of these debts for the past seven years, available credit, and a record of credit inquiries for the last two years. Negative credit information remains on your credit report for up to seven years; bankruptcy can remain for ten years. Your credit score is calculated using a variety of factors, including the number of credit cards you have, your total credit limit, the amount you own on accounts, and your past promptness in paying bills.

When you begin applying for financial aid, it's probably a good idea to get a copy of your credit report. You can obtain the report from the following national credit reporting agencies: Equifax (www.equifax.com; 800-997-2493, toll-free), Experian (www.experian.com; 800-422-4870, toll-free), and TransUnion (www.tuc.com; 800-888-4213, toll-free). If you have been denied credit within the past sixty days, you can obtain a free copy of your credit report. Otherwise, you will probably be charged a fee. Because you don't know which credit reporting agency that your lender will be requesting its information from, you may want to request your credit report from all three organizations. When you receive your credit reports, review them carefully for inaccuracies, and point these out to the reporting agency. They will investigate any problems and rectify your credit report, if necessary.

> **If you have at least one credit card, a car loan, undergraduate student loans, or any other type of personal credit, you've got a credit history.**

HOW MUCH MONEY WILL I NEED?

Before you determine how much money that you'll need to make it through business school, the first step is to get a clear understanding of your current financial status and the financial commitments that you already have. If you have outstanding undergraduate loans, you must understand the nature of the loans, the total that you owe, and the amount of interest that has accrued. If you have car loans, credit card loans, or other consumer debt, you need to understand what your repayment obligations are regarding these loans and how they will affect your ability to handle more debt.

Calculating Your Need

Step One: Identify all available financial resources. You can use the following guidelines, adapted from www.accessgroup.org.

Anticipated income (net annual income from
your employment and spouse's employment):_____

Other resources (savings and parent contributions,
gifts and other sources):_____

*Total Resources Available While Attending Business School:*_____

Step Two: Calculate the amount of direct educational expenses that you'll incur each year at every school to which you're applying.

Tuition:_____

Fees:_____

Books and supplies:_____

*Total educational expenses per year:*_____

Step Three: Calculate your yearly living expenses. If you are looking at schools in different parts of the country, be sure to take the cost of living in each location into consideration. Rent (and food, entertainment, and clothing) in New York City will, of course, be much higher than rent in the Midwest; don't forget this when you're looking at your total need package.

Rent (or rooming fees at the university,
if you're choosing that option):_____

Basic personal living expenses per month
(utilities, food, laundry, transportation, insurance):_____

Other personal expenses per month
(loan payments, dependent care expenses,
clothing, prescriptions, household goods and
furnishings, travel, car maintenance, etc.):_____

Miscellaneous expenses per month (recreation/
entertainment, interview expenses, gifts, etc):_____

Multiply by 12:_____

*Total yearly living expenses:*_____

Now, add the numbers from steps two and three together, and subtract that total from step one. Yikes! Now you see why financial aid is so important. As award packages come in from each of the schools to which you've applied, go back to the final totals you arrived at here. Subtract the amount of aid that you've been awarded from these totals. What do the numbers say? Will you need to take out a huge private loan to make ends meet while you attend school? If so, do you think it's worth it?

Remember, tuition fees alone give you only part of the picture when it comes to the amount of financial aid that you'll need to get through graduate school. As an undergraduate, once you paid your tuition and room and board, you were pretty much taken care of—except for the occasional pizza or round of drinks at the town pub. That's far from true when it comes to graduate school. As an adult, you've incurred more responsibilities—and the debt that goes with them. If you have a family of your own, there's even more to consider.

Can I Really Afford This?

If you've decided that you need to take out a loan to finance your business degree, you should determine whether you'll be able to repay it once you graduate. When making this determination, consider the following:

(1) *Your monthly student loan payment.* More important than your total indebtedness upon graduating is whether or not you'll be able to

Before you determine how much money you'll need to make it through business school, the first step is to get a clear understanding of your current financial status and the financial commitments that you already have.

pay the monthly loan installments. You can use Access Group's Access Advisor software, which features an interactive loan calculator, to help you project monthly payments.

(2) *Estimated future expenses.* Your budget after school will include most of the same components as your in-school budget, except, of course, your education expenses. Remember that you will probably have new expenses related to your job (clothing and transportation, for example), as well as the added expense of any undergraduate loans that you may have deferred while in graduate school.

(3) *Estimated starting salary.* Hooray! Once you get your business degree, you can finally get that high-paying job that you've been dreaming about. Be conservative with your estimates, however. Check average starting salaries for recent graduates in your field—and in the geographic location in which you think you'll be working.

After subtracting your future expenses and estimated student loan payment from your projected monthly income, you should be able to determine if you can afford your student loans. If you come out on the plus side after crunching these numbers, you probably can. If you have a zero balance, you'll have just enough to cover your post–graduate school lifestyle. If you come out in the red, you may need to reevaluate the amount you plan to borrow.

A Few Words about Budgeting

To avoid leaving business school with huge amounts of debt, you'll probably have to establish a detailed budget and stick to it. As little as any of us like to do this, sometimes budgeting is a necessity. When planning your budget, consider different cost-cutting measures. If you're not married, you may want to get a roommate, and you definitely have to think about reducing your entertainment expenses (yes, you probably should learn how to cook). You may find that public transportation is cheaper than owning a car. If you're attending business school full-time, save money while working during breaks. Above all, don't take on any further debt; resist the urge to pay for everything with plastic.

Think back to how you romanticized life as a graduate student before you realized how much it cost. Now you know that there's a reason why graduate students hang around in coffee shops a lot; they can't afford to go anywhere else! If you always keep your goals in mind, pinching pennies won't be as painful. In a few years, when you're at the head of the conference table directing a meeting on your company's next big project, you won't even remember all the peanut butter you had to eat to get there.

APPENDIX A: CONTACTS FOR AID IN YOUR STATE

ALABAMA

Alabama Commission on Higher Education, Suite 205, 3465 Norman Bridge Road, Montgomery, Alabama 36105-2310, Telephone 334-281-1998; or State Department of Education, Gordon Persons Office Building, 50 North Ripley Street, Montgomery, Alabama 36130-3901; Telephone 205-242-8082

ALASKA

Alaska Commission on Postsecondary Education, 3030 Vintage Boulevard, Juneau, Alaska 99801-7109; Telephone 907-465-2967; or State Department of Education, Goldbelt Place, 801 West 10th Street, Suite 200, Juneau, Alaska 99801-1894; Telephone 907-465-8715

ARIZONA

Arizona Commission for Postsecondary Education, 2020 North Central Ave., Suite 275, Phoenix, Arizona 85004-4503; Telephone 602-229-2531; or State Department of Education, 1535 West Jefferson, Phoenix, Arizona 85007; Telephone 602-542-2147

ARKANSAS

Arkansas Department of Higher Education, 114 East Capitol, Little Rock, Arkansas 72201-3818; Telephone 501-324-9300; or Arkansas Department of Education, 4 State Capitol Mall, Room 304A, Little Rock, Arkansas 72201-1071; Telephone 501-682-4474

CALIFORNIA

California Student Aid Commission; mailing address: P.O. Box 419026, Rancho Cordova, California 95741-9026; street address: California Student Aid Commission, 3300 Zinfandel Drive, Rancho Cordova, California 95670; Telephone 916-526-7590; or California Department of Education, 721 Capitol Mall, Sacramento, California 95814; Telephone 916-657-2451

COLORADO

Colorado Commission on Higher Education, Colorado Heritage Center, 1300 Broadway, 2nd Floor, Denver, Colorado 80203; Telephone 303-866-2723; State Department of Education, 201 East Colfax Avenue, Denver, Colorado 80203-1705; Telephone 303-866-6779

CONNECTICUT

Connecticut Department of Higher Education, 61 Woodland Street, Hartford, Connecticut 06105-2326; Telephone 860-947-1855; or Connecticut Department of Education, 165 Capitol Avenue, P.O. Box 2219, Hartford, Connecticut 06106-1630

DELAWARE

Delaware Higher Education Commission, Carvel State Office Building, Fourth Floor, 820 North French Street, Wilmington, Delaware 19801; Telephone 302-577-3240; or State Department of Public Instruction, Townsend Building #279, Federal and Lockerman Streets, P.O. Box 1402, Dover, Delaware 19903-1402; Telephone 302-739-4583

DISTRICT OF COLUMBIA

Department of Human Services, Office of Postsecondary Education, Research and Assistance, 2100 Martin Luther King, Jr., Avenue, SE, Suite 401, Washington, D.C. 20020; Telephone 202-727-3685; or District of Columbia Public Schools, Division of Student Services, 4501 Lee Street, NE, Washington, D.C. 20019; Telephone 202-724-4934

FLORIDA

Florida Department of Education, Office of Student Financial Assistance, 1344 Florida Education Center, 325 West Gaines Street, Tallahassee, Florida 32399-0400; Telephone 904-487-0649

GEORGIA

Georgia Student Finance Commission, State Loans and Grants Division, Suite 245, 2082 East Exchange Place, Tucker, Georgia 30084; Telephone 404-414-3000; or State Department of Education, 2054 Twin Towers East, 205 Butler Street, Atlanta, Georgia 30334-5040; Telephone 404-656-5812

HAWA2

Hawaii State Postsecondary Education Commission, 2444 Dole Street, Room 202, Honolulu, Hawaii 96822-2394; Telephone 808-956-8213; or Hawaii Department of Education, 2530 10th Avenue, Room A12, Honolulu, Hawaii 96816; Telephone 808-733-9103

IDAHO

Idaho Board of Education, P.O. Box 83720, Boise, Idaho 83720-0037; Telephone 208-334-2270; or State Department of Education, 650 West State Street, Boise, Idaho 83720; Telephone 208-334-2113

ILLINOIS

Illinois Student Assistance Commission, 1755 Lake Cook Road, Deerfield, Illinois 60015-5209; Telephone 708-948-8500

INDIANA

State Student Assistance Commission of Indiana, Suite 500, 150 West Market Street, Indianapolis, Indiana 46204-2811; Telephone 317-232-2350; or Indiana Department of Education, Room 229-State House, Center for Schools Improvement and Performance, Indianapolis, Indiana 46204-2798; Telephone 317-232-2305

IOWA

Iowa College Student Aid Commission, 914 Grand Avenue, Suite 201, Des Moines, Iowa 50309-2824; Telephone 800-383-4222

KANSAS

Kansas Board of Regents, 700 S.W. Harrison, Suite 1410, Topeka, Kansas 66603-3760; Telephone 913-296-3517; or State Department of Education, Kansas State Education Building, 120 East Tenth Street, Topeka, Kansas 66612; Telephone 913-296-4876

KENTUCKY

Kentucky Higher Education Assistance Authority, Suite 102, 1050 U.S. 127 South, Frankfort, Kentucky 40601-4323; Telephone 800-928-8926; or State Department of Education, 500 Mero Street, 1919 Capital Plaza Tower, Frankfort, Kentucky 40601, Telephone 502 564-3421

LOUISIANA

Louisiana Student Financial Assistance Commission, Office of Student Financial Assistance, P.O. Box 91202, Baton Rouge, Louisiana 70821-9202; Telephone 800-259-5626; or State Department of Education, P.O. Box 94064, 626 North 4th Street, 12th Floor, Baton Rouge, Louisiana 70804-9064; Telephone 504-342-2098

MAINE

Finance Authority of Maine, P.O. Box 949, Augusta, Maine 04333-0949; Telephone 207-287-3263; or Maine Department of Education, 23 State House Station, Augusta, Maine 04333-0023; Telephone for Voice: 207-287-5800, TDD/TTY for deaf and hard-of-hearing students: 207-287-2550

MARYLAND

Maryland Higher Education Commission, Jeffrey Building, 16 Francis Street, Annapolis, Maryland 21401-1781; Telephone 410-974-2971; or Maryland State Department of Education, 200 West Baltimore Street, Baltimore, Maryland 21201-2595; Telephone 410-767-0480

MASSACHUSETTS

Massachusetts Board of Higher Education, 330 Stuart Street, Boston, Massachusetts 02116; Telephone 617-727-9420; or State Department of Education, 350 Main Street, Malden, Massachusetts 02148-5023; Telephone 617-388-3300l; Massachusetts Higher Education Information Center, 676 Boylston St., Boston, Massachusetts 20116; Telephone 617-536-0200

MICHIGAN

Michigan Higher Education Assistance Authority, Office of Scholarships and Grants, P.O. Box 30462, Lansing, Michigan 48909-7962; Telephone 517-373-3394; or Michigan Department of Education, 608 West Allegan Street, Hannah Building, Lansing, Michigan 48909; Telephone 517-373-3324

MINNESOTA

Minnesota Higher Education Services Office, Suite 400, Capitol Square Bldg., 550 Cedar Street, St. Paul, Minnesota 55101-2292; Telephone 800-657-3866; or Department of Children, Families, and Learning, 712 Capitol Square Building, 550 Cedar Street, St. Paul, Minnesota 55101; Telephone 612-296-6104

MISSISSIPPI

Mississippi Postsecondary Education Financial Assistance Board, 3825 Ridgewood Road, Jackson, Mississippi 39211-6453; Telephone 601-982-6663; or State Department of Education, P.O. Box 771, Jackson, Mississippi 39205-0771; Telephone 601-359-3768

MISSOURI

Missouri Coordinating Board for Higher Education, 3515 Amazonas Drive, Jefferson City, Missouri 65109-5717; Telephone 314-751-2361; or Missouri State Department of Elementary and Secondary Education, P.O. Box 480, 205 Jefferson Street, Jefferson City, Missouri 65102-0480; Telephone 314-751-2931

MONTANA

Montana University System, 2500 Broadway, Helena, Montana 59620-3103; Telephone 406-444-6570; or State Office of Public Instruction, State Capitol, Room 106, Helena, Montana 59620; Telephone 406-444-4422

NEBRASKA

Coordinating Commission for Postsecondary Education, P.O. Box 95005, Lincoln, Nebraska 68509-5005; Telephone 402-471-2847; or Nebraska Department of Education, P.O. Box 94987, 301 Centennial Mall South, Lincoln, Nebraska 68509-4987; Telephone 402-471-2784

NEVADA

Nevada Department of Education, 400 West King Street, Capitol Complex, Carson City, Nevada 89710; Telephone 702-687-5915

NEW HAMPSHIRE

New Hampshire Postsecondary Education Commission, 2 Industrial Park Drive, Concord, New Hampshire 03301-8512; Telephone 603-271-2555; or State Department of Education, State Office Park South, 101 Pleasant Street, Concord, New Hampshire 03301; Telephone 603-271-2632

NEW JERSEY

State of New Jersey Office of Student Financial Assistance, 4 Quaker-bridge Plaza, CN 540, Trenton, New Jersey 08625; Telephone 800-792-8670; or State Department of Education, 225 West State Street, Trenton, New Jersey 08625-0500; Telephone 609-984-6409

NEW MEXICO

New Mexico Commission on Higher Education, 1068 Cerrillos Road, Santa Fe, New Mexico 87501-4925; Telephone 505-827-7383; or State Department of Education, Education Building, 300 Don Gaspar, Santa Fe, New Mexico 87501-2786; Telephone 505-827-6648

NEW YORK

New York State Higher Education Services Corporation, One Commerce Plaza, Albany, New York 12255; Telephone 518-474-5642; or State Education Department, 111 Education Building, Washington Avenue, Albany, New York 12234; Telephone 518-474-5705

NORTH CAROLINA

North Carolina State Education Assistance Authority, P.O. Box 2688, Chapel Hill, North Carolina 27515-2688; Telephone 919-821-4771; or State Department of Public Instruction, Education Building, Division of Teacher Education, 116 West Edenton Street, Raleigh, North Carolina 27603-1712; Telephone 919-733-0701

NORTH DAKOTA

North Dakota University System, North Dakota Student Financial Assistance Program, 600 East Boulevard Avenue, Bismarck, North Dakota 58505-0230; Telephone 701-224-4114; or State Department of Public Instruction, State Capitol Building, 11th Floor, 600 East Boulevard Avenue, Bismarck, North Dakota 58505-0164; Telephone 701-224-2271

OHIO

Ohio Board of Regents, P.O. Box 182452, 309 South Fourth Street, Columbus, Ohio 43218-2452; Telephone 888-833-1133 (toll-free); or State Department of Education, 65 South Front Street, Room 1005, Columbus, Ohio 43266-0308; Telephone 614-466-2761

OKLAHOMA

Oklahoma State Regents for Higher Education, Oklahoma Guaranteed Student Loan Program, P.O. Box 3000, Oklahoma City, Oklahoma 73101-3000; Telephone 800-247-0420 (toll-free); or State Department of Education, Oliver Hodge Memorial Education Building, 2500 North Lincoln Boulevard, Oklahoma City, Oklahoma 73105-4599; Telephone 405-521-4122

OREGON

Oregon State Scholarship Commission, Suite 100, 1500 Valley River Drive, Eugene, Oregon 97401-2130; Telephone 503-687-7400; or Oregon State System of Higher Education, 700 Pringle Parkway SE, Salem, Oregon 97310-0290; Telephone 503-378-5585; or Oregon Department of Education, 255 Capitol Street NE, Salem, Oregon 97310-0203

PENNSYLVANIA

Pennsylvania Higher Education Assistance Agency, 1200 North Seventh Street, Harrisburg, Pennsylvania 17102-1444; Telephone 800-692-7435

RHODE ISLAND

Rhode Island Board of Governors for Higher Education & Rhode Island Office of Higher Education, 301 Promenade Street, Providence, Rhode Island 02908-5720; Telephone 401-277-6560; or Rhode Island

Higher Education Assistance Authority, 560 Jefferson Boulevard, Warwick, Rhode Island 02886: Telephone 800-922-9855; or State Department of Education, 22 Hayes Street, Providence, Rhode Island 02908; Telephone 401-277-3126

SOUTH CAROLINA

South Carolina Higher Education Tuition Grants Commission, 1310 Lady Street, Suite 811, P.O. Box 12159, Columbia, South Carolina 29201; Telephone 803-734-1200; or State Department of Education, 803A Rutledge Building, 1429 Senate Street, Columbia, South Carolina 29201; Telephone 803-734-8364

SOUTH DAKOTA

Department of Education and Cultural Affairs, Office of the Secretary, 700 Governors Drive, Pierre, South Dakota 57501-2291; Telephone 605 773-3134

TENNESSEE

Tennessee Higher Education Commission, 404 James Robertson Parkway, Suite 1900, Nashville, Tennesee 37243-0820; Telephone 615-741-3605; or State Department of Education, 100 Cordell Hull Building, Nashville, Tennessee 37219-5335; Telephone 800-342-1663

TEXAS

Texas Higher Education Coordinating Board, P.O. Box 12788, Capitol Station, Austin, Texas 78711; Telephone 800-242-3062

UTAH

Utah State Board of Regents, Utah System of Higher Education, 355 West North Temple, #3 Triad Center, Suite 550, Salt Lake City, Utah 84180-1205; Telephone 801-321-7205; or Utah State Office of Education, 250 East 500 South, Salt Lake City, Utah 84111; Telephone 801-538-7779

VERMONT

Vermont Student Assistance Corporation, Champlain Mill, P.O. Box 2000, Winooski, Vermont 05404-2601; Telephone 800-642-3177 (toll-free); or Vermont Department of Education, 120 State Street, Montpelier, Vermont 05620-2501; Telephone 802-828-3147

VIRGINIA

State Council of Higher Education for Virginia, James Monroe Building, 101 North Fourteenth Street, Richmond, Virginia 23219; Telephone 804-786-1690; or State Department of Education, P.O. Box 2120, James Monroe Building, 14th and Franklin Streets, Richmond, Virginia 23216-2120; Telephone 804-225-2072

WASHINGTON

Washington State Higher Education Coordinating Board, P.O. Box 43430, 917 Lakeridge Way SW, Olympia, Washington 98504-3430; Telephone 206-753-7850; or State Department of Public Instruction, Old Capitol Building, P.O. Box FG 11, Olympia, Washington 98504-3211; Telephone 206-753-2858

WEST VIRGINIA

State Department of Education, 1900 Washington Street, Building B, Room 358, Charleston, West Virginia 25305; Telephone 304-588-2691; or State College & University Systems of West Virginia Central Office, 1018 Kanawha Boulevard East, Suite 700, Charleston, West Virginia 25301-2827; Telephone 304-558-4016

WISCONSIN

Higher Educational Aids Board, P.O. Box 7885, Madison, Wisconsin 53707-7885; Telephone 608-267-2206; or State Department of Public Instruction, 125 South Wester Street, P.O. Box 7841, Madison, Wisconsin 53707-7814; Telephone 608-266-2364

WYOMING

Wyoming State Department of Education, Hathaway Building, 2300 Capitol Avenue, 2nd Floor, Cheyenne, Wyoming 82002-0050; Telephone 307-777-6265

APPENDIX B: SELECT LIST OF SOURCES OF AID

Note to readers: This list is printed here as a way to get you started in your search for financial aid opportunities; it is by no means exhaustive. As a second step, consult Appendix 2 at the end of this book for more resources.

Loans That Are Meant Specifically for Business Students and Graduate Students

Several lending institutions offer loans that are meant especially for business students and graduate students. You may want to check out Access Group's Business Access Loan (www.accessgroup.org), Key Bank's MBAchiever and GradAchiever loans (www.key.com), Nellie Mae's MBA-EXCEL and GradExcel loans (www.nelliemae.com), Sallie Mae's MBA LOANS (www.salliemae.com), the Education Resources Institute's Professional Education Plan (PEP) loans (www.teri.org), and Citibank's MBAAssist Loan (www.citibank.com).

Aid for International Students

Aid for international graduate students is scarce, but two good resources will get your search started: *Scholarships for Study in the USA and Canada* (Princeton, NJ: Peterson's, 1998) and *Funding for U.S. Study—A Guide for International Students and Professionals*, by Carol Weeg, Ellen Stern, and Jim Bauer (Princeton, NJ: Institute for International Education, 1996).

Norwest Bank offers loans to international students studying business; for more information, write to Norwest Bank/HEMAR Insurance Corporation., GMAC, 2400 Broadway, Suite 320, Santa Monica, California 90404-3064. The TERI PEP loan is also available to international students; find out more at www.teri.org.

Aid for Women

The American Association of University Women (AAUW) offers direct support to women through fellowships, grants, and awards. For information about AAUW scholarships and fellowships, contact the AAUW Educational Foundation, 2201 North Dodge Street, Iowa City, Iowa 52243-4030 (Telephone 319-337-1716).

The Business and Professional Women's Foundation (BPW) maintains a list of scholarships and fellowships that are aimed at women age 30 and over who are going back to school to upgrade their career skills, train for a new career, or reenter the job market. To find out more, write to Scholarships, BPW Foundation, 2012 Massachusetts Avenue NW, Washington, DC 20036.

Women In Defense (WID) has established its HORIZONS Scholarship Foundation to assist women who are pursuing, or plan to pursue, careers related to U.S. national security. Applicants must be U.S. citizens, have a minimum GPA of 3.25, and be studying business, engineering, law, international relations, economics, computer science, physics, operations research, mathematics, or other fields relevant to a career in the area of national security or defense. For more information, write to HORIZONS Application, c/o WID, 2101 Wilson Boulevard, Suite 400, Arlington, Virginia 22201-3061.

Aid for Minority Students

The Consortium for Graduate Study in Management, a group of eleven universities, offers full-tuition fellowships to African American, Native American, and Hispanic U.S. citizens for graduate study leading to a master's degree in business; more than 180 are awarded annually. Contact the Consortium for Graduate Study in Management, 200 South Hanley Road, Suite 1102, St. Louis, Missouri 63015; Telephone 313-935-5614, e-mail cgsm@wuolin.wustl.edu.

African American students searching for aid can contact Black Excel for a list of more than 350 grants and scholarships. For information, write to them at 28 Vesey Street, Suite 2239, New York, New York 10007, or call 718-527-8896.

HyperAMP is a set of programs and resource guides for minority students produced by the Hispanic Research Center at Arizona State University. For more information, contact HyperAMP/Aid, c/o Hispanic Research Center, Box 87272, Arizona State University, Tempe, Arizona 85287-2702.

Advice from Admissions Directors

In this chapter, admissions directors from ten schools give you their perspective on the value of an advanced degree in business, what you should look for when choosing a business program, and what they look for when reviewing business school applications. To gather responses, we asked business school admissions officers around the world to respond to an e-mail questionnaire; those who responded are included here. Admissions officers responded to as many questions as they chose of those that were posed:

- When is the right time for prospective students to start thinking about business school? Upon graduating from college? After a few years in the job market? Why?
- What is the value of an advanced degree in business—in today's society and in the future?
- What are the most important factors that a prospective student should consider when researching business programs? Some of these could include future career plans; reputation of faculty and school; cost of program; geographic location; availability of part-time, full-time, and distance options; and so on.
- How heavily does your program weigh the following admissions criteria? (1) undergraduate grades, (2) GMAT scores, (3) work experience, (4) letters of recommendation, and (5) essays. Why do you place the emphasis where you do?
- Speaking particularly of essays, how many essays does your program require the student to write? What kinds of questions do you ask? In your opinion, what makes the difference between a good essay and a bad one? What do you look for when you read admissions essays?
- Speaking particularly of work experience, what kind of work experience do you look for? Does it necessarily have to be in a business field?

- Speaking particularly of letters of recommendation, what advice would you give students about whom to ask to write recommendations?

- When you look at transcripts, do undergraduate business majors have an advantage over those with majors in other fields? If someone's major wasn't in a business or related field (economics, for example), what would your advice be to them?

- How important is timing in the admissions process? In other words, do students who apply early have an advantage over those who just meet the deadlines?

- Finally, what words of wisdom do you have for students who are considering applying to business school? This can cover any topic that you wish.

To round out the admissions officers' statements, we've also gathered key facts and figures about each program to give you a more complete picture of each institution. With the exception of Yale University, the data for each institution were collected by Peterson's survey of M.B.A. programs, 1999.

▶Julie R. Barefoot

Assistant Dean of Admissions and Career
  Management
Goizueta Business School, Emory University

Fast Facts about the Business School

Location: Atlanta, Georgia

Enrollment: 560 (360 full-time, 200 part-time)

Degrees offered: M.B.A., Executive M.B.A., dual M.B.A./Doctor of
  Jurisprudence (J.D.), dual M.B.A./Master of Public Health
  (M.B.A./M.P.H.), dual M.B.A./Master of Divinity (M.Div.)

Average age: 27

Web site: www.emory.edu/BUS

It is ideal if candidates begin considering business school while they are
still in college. By doing so, they can begin to prepare by taking courses,
such as business statistics and/or calculus. This is beneficial because
such courses help students to develop analytical skills—even if they
aren't business, math, or science majors. Also, it is typically easier to
take these classes while in college, when one's quantitative skills are still
strong. Along those lines, I encourage college seniors to take the
GMAT prior to graduation. The test is valid for five years, and most
applicants apply to business school within this time frame. Again, this
usually helps an applicant because most individuals do not use the math
skills that they learned in college when they are on the job.

Since I have an M.B.A. myself (University of North Carolina, '83)
and have worked in admissions at Goizueta since 1988, I obviously feel
passionately about the long-term value of the M.B.A. degree. I could
speak about this topic for hours, but in a nutshell, the beauty of the
M.B.A. degree is that it teaches you the business analytical skills that
you need to operate in today's global business environment. The
M.B.A. degree gives candidates the tools needed to address business
problems and also the confidence to take on challenges at work. Our
M.B.A. program is particularly strong in exposing candidates to the
international perspective so critical in making business decisions;
Goizueta also immerses them in the technological aspects of business
operations today, and our faculty members share with them what they

The M.B.A. is an amazingly flexible degree because it gives its holders the ability to transition between positions and industries.

can anticipate in the years ahead. The M.B.A. is an amazingly flexible degree because it gives its holders the ability to transition between positions and industries. Just this week, I've received e-mails from two different M.B.A. alumni who previously were working in brand management roles in the consumer product industry; now they're both moving to e-business firms to work on corporate marketing strategies!

In judging prospective students' applications, the most important factor we look for is the quality of their work experience. Because our program is highly interactive, we expect that students will learn as much from classroom discussions and group work as they will from faculty lectures. Clearly, the only way that this will happen is if each applicant brings something to the table in terms of enriching our program's classroom experience. A close second in terms of our review process is our assessment of the applicant's ability to perform well academically in our program. Our program is rigorous and requires not only strong quantitative skills (as demonstrated in the GMAT quantitative score and in grades received on any quantitative course work, such as statistics or calculus) but also the ability to effectively juggle multiple courses and group projects. Candidates' undergraduate transcripts give us a track record of how they perform in an academic setting as well as a sense of their preparation for analytical work and of their leadership experiences; we very much like to see evidence of extracurricular activity and personal initiative in college and afterward.

You may rightly ask where the essays, interview, and letters of recommendation fit into this process. These components are also key pieces of the puzzle. Essays give us more information about the applicant's work responsibilities as well as a sense of what they might contribute to class discussions. Letters of recommendation give us firsthand insight into how the candidate is regarded either in a work or a social setting—again, critical information for the admissions committee to consider. Our program strongly recommends a personal interview so that we can gain a much clearer picture of the applicant's interpersonal skills and the quality of his or her work experience by asking more in-depth questions about career progression and challenges. All of this data is reviewed so that we can make the best decision possible for the applicant and Goizueta.

At a minimum, an applicant's essays should answer the question posed on the application. Goizueta asks four questions. The first relates to the applicant's most significant experience. For this question, we expect the applicant to discuss a work-related example; it is not viewed favorably if the applicant discusses something that happened in college, unless it was extraordinary (a fraternity presidency or the like, for example, is *not* considered extraordinary). The second question asks the applicant to discuss his or her post-M.B.A. plans and the remaining two essays are one-page sentence completions such as: "My family is unique because . . ." or "The greatest lesson I have learned is . . ." In addition to answering the questions, the essays should be grammatically well-written and well-organized and should have a strong and/or thoughtful conclusion. In the essays, we look for a deeper sense of the applicant's personality, and we like to see some "spark"—a sense of humor and some insightful comments about what applicants have learned on the job, in their family life, or through their collegiate studies, for example. Goizueta students are known for wanting to "make a difference," and we look for evidence of that in the applicant's prior life experiences.

We have a very diverse class in terms of the work experience they bring—when we evaluate an applicant's work experience, we're not looking for a specific type of job, but we do look for the following: evidence of career progression (in other words, is this person valued at their company, and has he or she been given more responsibility since beginning employment?) and evidence that the job was responsible and in some sense required the use of good organizational or strategic thinking skills. Clearly, if the job required strong analytical skills, that is a plus. Applicants should know that a great deal depends on how they explain their work experience in their essays and personal interview and how their letters of recommendation (if they are work-related) confirm the quality of their work. At Goizueta, we have candidates with engineering backgrounds, candidates who are CPAs, candidates who have worked for the Peace Corps, candidates who are AIDS researchers, candidates who are pharmaceutical sales reps, and candidates who are financial analysts—we value many, many types of work experience.

Applicants whose undergraduate background is not in business are not at a disadvantage in the admissions process. I say that with the

> **When discussing work-related experience, it is not viewed favorably if the applicant discusses something that happened in college, unless it was extraordinary. A fraternity presidency for example, is *not* considered extraordinary.**

following caveat: liberal arts majors who did not take quantitative course work must fully demonstrate (through the GMAT quantitative score or a statistics course grade) that they can handle the rigor of the analytical courses that they'll take in business school. Obviously, when we review the transcript of a business major, they will have a number of quantitative classes that we can review (in addition to the GMAT) when making this assessment.

The timing of an application is not critically important at Goizueta, meaning that we try very hard to be consistent throughout the selection process. Having said that, if applicants want to be reviewed for the merit-based scholarships that we offer, they must apply by our scholarship deadline (February 15) or risk seriously damaging their opportunity for a full review for these awards.

My words of wisdom? Seriously consider the programs to which you apply; remember, you will be working intimately with these classmates for the duration of your program of study, and they will become your network for your business career. I urge candidates to look beyond rankings numbers and to visit the program and experience the learning and living environment being offered.

►James Culbertson

Assistant Director of Recruitment and Admissions,
  MBA Program
Graduate School of Business Administration
University of Colorado at Boulder

Fast Facts about the Business School

Location: Boulder, Colorado

Enrollment: 265 (150 full-time, 115 part-time)

Degrees offered: Master of Business Administration (M.B.A.), dual
  M.B.A./Master of Science (M.S.) in telecommunications, dual
  M.B.A./Doctor of Jurisprudence (J.D.), Master of Science
(M.S.)   in business administration

Average age: 30

Web site: www-bus.colorado.edu

Quite frankly, it is never too early for prospective students to start thinking about business school. While it is true that most M.B.A. programs today require some level of postgraduate experience, there are certainly several areas that a prospective student can begin addressing while still in their undergraduate program, primarily academic credentials such as GPA. This is really their only opportunity to dramatically impact their GPA, and addressing this issue now can help them avoid having to spend time on an application explaining, or rationalizing, a low GPA. Also, if the goal is to attend business school within a few years of completing the undergraduate degree, it can make sense to take the GMAT while still in school or soon after completion. This allows the prospective applicant to take advantage of being in the "student" frame of mind, that is, used to studying and taking tests. Scores are valid for five years, so this does give a window of time to acquire some work experience and begin applying to business schools. I would recommend beginning the application process for business school up to a year in advance, as this will allow the applicant to address any apparent deficiencies in their application. Also, the decision to attend business school should not be taken lightly. Business school requires considerable commitment, both of time and money. Applicants should allow themselves an adequate period of time to sort through the variety of options that are available to them and make an informed decision that best fits their individual needs.

Simply put, an M.B.A. is a professional degree, designed to prepare its holder for higher-level positions requiring strategic decision-making that can impact the organization as a whole. Earning an M.B.A. can lead to positions of great responsibility, with accompanying financial reward.

I would encourage applicants to strongly consider their future career plans when weighing which programs to consider. The most important thing is to select programs that will meet the applicant's professional development needs. If the goal is work at an investment bank on Wall Street, for example, then the applicant should choose from the small subset of programs that serve as feeder schools for that particular market.

If the goal is to attend business school within a few years of completing the undergraduate degree, it can make sense to take the GMAT while still in school or soon after completion.

In our admissions evaluation, we tend to place the greatest weight on work experience and career goals, followed by GMAT scores, undergraduate grades, and letters of recommendation. We also are asking how the applicant will add value to the experience of their classmates. It is certainly important that an applicant demonstrate the academic ability necessary to be successful in the program. A strong performance on the GMAT is definitely an eye-catcher in the admissions process. It is more important, however, that applicants demonstrate the potential for professional success upon completion of the program. It also important that applicants "fit" with the program. This means that their development goals should mesh with what the program has to offer. Programs have different strengths and placement niches. We are simply not going to admit someone, regardless of their academic credentials, if we don't feel we can help facilitate their professional development and assist them in taking the next step in their career.

We currently ask applicants to provide four essays. The essays address applicants' professional experiences to date and how these experiences have led them to decide to pursue an M.B.A., how an M.B.A. will augment their professional development, and the decisions that they have made that have hindered or enhanced their professional growth. A good essay demonstrates clear, analytical thinking; the ability to honestly self-assess; and a plan of attack for the applicant's professional future. While we will interview any applicant we are considering admitting, the essays are applicants' primary opportunity to convince us to pass them on to this next step in the evaluation process.

The applicant's work experience should have led them to the decision to pursue an M.B.A. While the experience does not have to be in a business field, ideally it will have some relevance to the direction in which the applicant plans to head after completing the program. For those making a career transition, it is important that they demonstrate how skills from their current portfolio will transfer to the new career direction, as well as what steps they will take while in the program to facilitate this transition.

Applicants should seek recommendations from individuals who can provide a solid testament to their potential for professional success. We are looking for students with demonstrated potential to manage and lead others, so ideally the person providing a recommendation should be able to address this area. I am often asked if it is acceptable to have a former professor provide a recommendation. I tend to discourage this, simply because we feel we have a pretty good understanding of the applicant's academic potential based on other aspects of the application. If the applicant worked with the professor on special projects or other work outside the classroom, then a recommendation from him or her might be acceptable. Applicants should bear in mind that we are using the recommendations to more closely address the issue of their potential for professional success.

We are not looking for a specific major when making admissions decisions. However, an applicant does need to demonstrate the ability to handle the program academically. Specifically, because the study of business is quite quantitative in nature, it is critical that an applicant demonstrate the ability to handle this sort of work. An applicant who has not completed any quantitative course work prior to beginning an M.B.A. program will oftentimes be at a disadvantage. In this case, we might recommend completing courses in mathematics (algebra and calculus), statistics, finance, and the like, prior to beginning the program.

> **A strong performance on the GMAT is definitely an eye-catcher in the admissions process. It is more important, however, that applicants demonstrate the potential for professional success upon completion of the program.**

www.petersons.com
Game Plan for Getting into Business School
111

From an admissions standpoint, if the applicant presents a strong quantitative percentile on the GMAT, it tends to mitigate any concerns we may have with their academic credentials.

For our program specifically, there currently is not an advantage in applying early. I would not, however, recommend waiting until our late deadline, since at that point we will be admitting on a space-available basis only.

Finally, I can't emphasize enough the importance of selecting the right program for your specific needs. Weigh your options carefully. Based on your career goals, the location of the school may be a critical question, if it is well-positioned within a certain geographic business region. A program will tend to "push" you toward its strengths, as well it should. However, if the direction a program will lead you in is not the direction you wish to head, you are probably better served not applying to that program.

▶Dr. Daniel M. Gropper

Assistant Dean and Executive Director, M.B.A. Programs
Auburn University College of Business

Fast Facts about the Business School

Location: Auburn University, Alabama
Enrollment: 347 (126 full-time, 221 part-time)
Degrees offered: Master of Business Administration (M.B.A.)
Average age: 27
Web site: www.mba.business.auburn.edu

While some people could reasonably consider an M.B.A. coming straight from an undergraduate program (particularly if they are in a technical undergraduate program), most people will get the greatest gain after a couple of years of full-time work. It helps to have a good focus on what you want the program to do for you, although you should be open to changes of plans while you are in school. Also, the focus and maturity provided by a couple of years in the work force are needed by most people.

With an advanced degree in business, you get a broad perspective on managing people and organizations. You are challenged to think innovatively and to consider points of view that will be new to you. An M.B.A. also typically enhances one's professional opportunities. The "return on investment" for many M.B.A. programs, in many cases particularly those outside the "elite" range, is generally very high.

What should you look at when researching business programs? In one word, *fit.* Does the program meet your needs? Do you feel comfortable when you talk to people from the school? Is the program likely to allow you to do the things you want to do? I also think one should consider any program based on the program's reputation and a return on investment calculation. Consider the cost of tuition, books, living expenses, and so on, as well as your lost earnings while in school. Then look at the differential between your earnings now and when you graduate. While money isn't everything, it is a shame to invest two years of your life, perhaps take out $60,000 in student loans, and maybe give up $80,000 to 100,000 in lost earnings if you are not going to improve your professional situation when you graduate.

With an advanced degree in business, you get a broad perspective on managing people and organizations. You are challenged to think innovatively and to consider points of view that will be new to you.

At Auburn, we weigh undergraduate grades fairly heavily, and we also consider the applicant's major and university or college attended. We actually prefer students from nonbusiness fields, particularly engineers. We also weigh GMAT scores, both verbal and quantitative, fairly heavily; we consider the AWA less so than the other scores. Work experience is considered less so than grades and GMAT scores, except for Executive M.B.A. students, for whom work experience is more critical. Exceptional work experience may cause an applicant to jump out, but not usually. Unless we know the source of an applicant's recommendations and they are unusually good, we don't weigh them as heavily as undergraduate grades and GMAT scores. And unless something in them is highly unusual, we don't place as much emphasis on essays as we do on grades, GMAT scores, and work experience.

Applicants write one essay, in which we ask them to discuss their goals, plans, and so on. We look for organization, focus, clear writing, and reasonableness. Bad essays are ones with "pat" answers and bad writing. Good essays are crisp, to the point, well-organized, and have reasonable, well-supported goals.

When looking for recommenders, ask someone who can say something specific about what you did. Avoid someone too high up in the organization just because they have a better title, unless you did something specific for that person. Avoid a letter from the CEO if it would be generic; for example, "Jane was a superb employee and a great person" doesn't really tell us too much. Far better is a recommendation with specific accomplishments and examples of superb performance.

When applying, avoid the last-minute rush, and make sure everything is in on time. Do not call and harass the secretaries about the status of your application.

Words of wisdom? "Begin with the end in mind." Not original with me, but still good advice. Know what you want to get out of this, and commit to doing what needs to be done. Be focused and work hard, but take time to have fun, too. Business school can be one of the most fun and challenging educational experiences of your life.

►Angela G. Gruber

Manager of Admissions
The Lake Forest Graduate School of Management

Fast Facts about the Business School

Location: Lake Forest, Illinois
Enrollment: 875 (875 part-time, 0 full-time)
Degree offered: Executive M.B.A.
Average age: 32
Web site: www.lfgsm.ed

I find that prospective students benefit the most when they start to consider graduate school after a few years in the work force. Students can begin their postgraduate work by gaining experience and learning to speak the business language. Students will have more to offer a business class when they have lived in the business world. Work experience also allows a student the opportunity to find their niche in the business world, which they can then expand upon with a graduate degree.

I see the graduate degree becoming what the bachelor's degree was twenty years ago—a requirement. In job advertisements, now you see "M.B.A. Preferred." That means that if you are one of ten applicants for the job and you are the only one without the M.B.A., your application will be eliminated. Graduate education has become an expectation in the business world for advancement. A person must meet the expectations laid out or they are left behind.

When evaluating a graduate school, I suggest that a prospective student ask what projects they will be working on in the program. Projects provide a working model where skills can be gained that will last a lifetime. They should also ask how much work experience the faculty has outside of the academic world. Then the prospective student should evaluate their lifestyle and determine what is important to them, for example, full-time versus part-time studies, cost, and geographic location, among other factors.

Lake Forest looks at students as a whole picture, not just as single elements. Our students are not the same people they were at 18 or 22 years old. They have gained important knowledge and education

We look at work experience broadly. If students can demonstrate responsibility, organizational skills, and leadership potential, we are open. Work experience can be anywhere, although the vast majority of the experience we see is in some sort of business field.

**Graduate
education has
become an
expectation in the
business world
for advancement.
A person must
meet the
expectations laid
out or they are
left behind.**

through their work and the natural progression of maturity. So we do emphasize their work experience and the letter of recommendation to show us how they work today. Then we look at transcripts and GMAT scores to see what kind of student they have been. The essay indicates writing style and motivation to be in the program. We look at every student to see what kind of potential they have to succeed in our program. Then we look at what our program can offer to them and what they can offer to the program.

We require our students to write one essay answering the question: "Why do you want to pursue an M.B.A. degree? Describe how this experience will affect your professional/personal development." When I read an essay, I read the content for motivation and an understanding of what graduate school means. I then look for a general understanding of grammar, sentence structure, spelling, and composition. How a student writes is as important as what they write.

▶Chris Hall

M.B.A. Director
Macquarie Graduate School of Management

Fast Facts about the Business School

Location: Sydney, Australia

Enrollment: 1,490

Degrees offered: Master of Business Administration (M.B.A.),
  Master of Management (M.Mgt.)

Average age: 34

Web site: www.gsm.mq.edu.au

When you begin your search for the right business program, you should really start by considering what *you* want. What are your needs, and why do you want an M.B.A.? An M.B.A. is a fairly big commitment in time and money. It may be that your needs would be better met by taking some very specific courses in a particular area (such as marketing or human resources management) so that you get a promotion quickly. Later on, you can move to a full M.B.A. if you need to. An M.B.A. is useful when you are moving up the ladder to become a more general manager, with oversight across different areas in the organization.

When you're looking at specific programs, you should consider:

1. The quality and reputation of the program. There are plenty of M.B.A. programs around—about forty in Australia alone. Some are better known and more readily recognized by employers than others. This is not to say that some are better than others; they may actually be better suited to your needs and budget. But be aware that not all M.B.A. programs are equal.

2. The quality of the staff. In some M.B.A. programs, the staff is shared with undergraduate programs; in others, like Macquarie, the staff is dedicated to postgraduate teaching. Will you be taught by junior tutors with little or no business experience or by senior staff with higher degrees and extensive industry experience? At Macquarie, there is a very high

proportion of senior staff, all have consulting and industry experience, many are doing leading-edge research, and most have Ph.D. degrees or are working toward them.

3. Teaching methods. A lot of M.B.A. programs teach material that is taught at undergraduate level—accounting, finance, management, and so on. Doing the same things again with the same quality of lecturers does not help you learn anything useful about management. A good M.B.A. program covers the material that is used in management and shows you how to *apply* it, by means of lectures, case studies, projects, simulations, etc. Ask how you will *learn* things and how you will apply them.

4. Other students. If all of the other students are straight out of undergraduate degrees, you will not learn much from them about management. At Macquarie, all students have at least five years of work experience and on average have about ten years. If you are working closely with other students in syndicate groups, working on cases and real problems, experience counts. You also learn a lot about dealing with organizational politics—something you do not learn much about in a distance program.

5. Flexibility. Can you plan ahead? Can you find out what timetable options are available twelve months or so in advance? Can you choose to attend classes on weekends, at nights, or in the morning? Can you defer study for a while or swap from full-time to part-time and vice versa so you can slow down or speed up your degree depending on your circumstances? If you get transferred abroad, can you continue studying?

6. Flexibility in tailoring your degree to your needs. When it comes to marketing yourself, it is important to make your degree stand out in the crowd. Can you take electives that allow you to specialize your degree? How much choice is there in electives? Can you carry out specific projects related to your career or to your employers' needs? For example, if you want to shift careers and move into a new company, it might be possible to carry out a project on that company and show the managers what you can really do.

7. Is the program up to date? Are subjects and the degree continually reviewed and kept up to date? For example, at Macquarie, we have just introduced three new updated electives in specialized areas of electronic commerce, competitive intelligence for global business, and best practices (the latter involves studying business firsthand in Europe and Asia). All main core subjects are regularly reviewed and upgraded.

8. Physical location and safety. These are important to women especially. Is there readily accessible safe transport—do you have secure parking and good security? M.B.A. classes and syndicate teams often work late at night.

9. Facilities. What is the quality of physical facilities? Are they comfortable, clean, and well-equipped with LCD projectors, computers, and Web connections? Do you share them with undergraduates? Can you get a decent, well-balanced, non-junk-food meal in a hurry?

10. What sort of career success does the program have? What networks does it offer? Because most Macquarie students are working while they get their degree, there is an immediate network of people you come in contact with that can help you identify opportunities for a career move. To this is added a global network of about 5,000 Macquarie graduates. We also provide free contact and advisory counseling services to help introduce you to potential employers, if you need it. A good program will be able to offer you all of these features.

Physical location and safety are important to women especially. Is there readily accessible safe transport—do you have secure parking and good security? M.B.A. classes and syndicate teams often work late at night.

►**Noory Lalji**
Coordinator, M.B.A. Program
Simon Fraser University

Fast Facts about the Business School

Location: Burnaby, Canada

Enrollment: 147 (147 full-time, 0 part-time)

Degrees offered: M.B.A., dual M.B.A./Master of Resource
   Management (M.R.M.)

Average age: 27

Web site: www.bus.sfu.ca

Students can begin thinking about furthering their education in a business school either upon graduating from college or after a few years in the job market. However, work experience does help students identify their future goals and provides a perspective on their educational needs.

In today's competitive society, an advanced education prepares students to deal with issues in a professional manner. Students with an advanced degree have an edge on other employees who have chosen not to further their education. As the business world becomes more complicated, formal business training will become more essential. For example, students in the M.B.A. program at Simon Fraser University (SMU) learn to deal with complex and strategic issues within uncertain and dynamic business environments through study in specialized areas. In this respect, the M.B.A. degree is certainly useful to all individuals.

The SFU M.B.A. program does not require students to write essays. However, importance is placed heavily on students' cumulative grade point average and GMAT scores. Letters of recommendation are important to judge the student's ability to perform well in the program, and a personal statement assists the Admissions Committee in deciding whether the student's future goals will be achieved at SFU. Work experience in a business field would certainly be useful to applicants to SFU's business program; however, the student's performance and his or her leadership quality in any job would also prove helpful in gaining

> **Work experience in a business field would certainly be useful to applicants to SFU's business program; however, the student's performance and his or her leadership quality in any job would also prove helpful for admission to the program.**

admission to the program. The program has a special form for referees. Out of the three letters of recommendation, two letters must be academic—either from their previous or present professors.

The SFU program admits only those students who have completed an undergraduate degree in business. However, non-business students are advised to complete a one-year diploma program on line (Graduate Diploma in Business Administration) before applying to the Specialist M.B.A. Program. The admission committee considers all applications received by the deadline. However, those students who apply early have an advantage in finding out in more timely manner on status of their admission. Therefore, it is beneficial to send in one's application as early as possible in order to ensure a spot in the program.

▶**Ruth Pechauer**
Associate Director, Marketing & Admissions
Carlson School of Management
University of Minnesota, Twin Cities Campus

Fast Facts about the Business School

Location: Minneapolis, Minnesota

Enrollment: 1,146 (282 full-time, 864 part-time)

Degrees offered: Master of Business Administration (M.B.A.), Master of Business Taxation (M.B.T.), Master of Arts (M.A.) in human resources and industrial relations, Master of Healthcare Administration (M.H.A.), Executive Development M.B.A. (E.M.B.A.), Master of Science (M.S.) in management of technology, Doctoral degrees (Ph.D.) in human resources and industrial relations and health service administration

Average age: 27

Web site: www.csom.umn.edu

The best time to start thinking about business school is when an individual has experienced a few years in the work force. Work experience gives individuals a context from which to understand concepts taught through textbooks and case studies. Individuals can also contribute much more to classroom discussion, which is often graded by professors. Indeed, part of the unique educational benefits from an M.B.A. program are the insights received from classmates who come from a variety of academic and work backgrounds. Finally, company recruiters generally prefer hiring an M.B.A. with prior work experience. Such candidates tend to have matured more quickly given their prior exposure to different management situations and their ability to understand the practical implications of theoretical concepts. On a more personal level, recent undergraduates often are not completely clear on career choices and opportunities. By allowing for some time in the work force, such aspects become clearer and the individual can make wiser choices when deciding upon one or two specializations within an M.B.A. degree.

An advanced degree in business not only looks at how decisions made in one functional area (e.g., finance) may effect operations in another functional area (e.g., marketing) but is also very much concerned with the latest business innovations and the effects of business decisions at the micro- and macro-environmental level. Students learn helpful models that provide flexible parameters for making decisions in changing economic and social environments.

When looking at programs, an individual should first narrow the many choices down to business schools that have strengths in disciplines important to his or her future career goals. The short list should not be limited to schools that make a ranking in any particular magazine, although such resources are a good place to start. However, such rankings can also detract one from thinking about other programs that are very strong and have other positive attributes to offer besides just the academic program. Second, the costs of programs vary considerably. Determine whether any financial aid is offered, graduate assistantships are available, and the degree of success students experience in finding jobs after graduation. Third, does the individual prefer an urban setting, and if so, what types of experiences are available with the business community? Is diversity of the business community important? Or would the individual prefer to deal with less distraction and focus more on studies? Is the reputation of the school more important than its particular strengths? Perhaps the company the individual wants to work for only recruits from certain business schools. One thing to keep in mind in this respect is that usually such programs are larger, and thus the competition for obtaining employment with such companies is more competitive.

In reviewing applications, we place equal weight on undergraduate grades, GMAT scores, work experience, letters of recommendation, and essays. Undergraduate grades and GMAT scores provide admission counselors with information on whether an applicant can perform well in a rigorous academic program. Work experience and essays provide insight to the level of responsibilities an applicant has been exposed to and the maturity level of the applicant's thought process in terms of goals, direction, and leadership. They also help determine the

A "bad" essay is vague and general, requiring little creative thought process. A "good" essay will give a sense of maturity and clear goals, showing that the person has gone through a careful thought process based on past experiences and knowledge about future opportunities.

contribution level, both in terms of depth and uniqueness, that the applicant has to offer to class discussion. Letters of recommendation provide further insight into an applicant's overall character and ability to work in teams.

Carlson School of Management requires three essays that touch on leadership, accomplishments, and goals. A "bad" essay is vague and general, requiring little creative thought process. A "good" essay will give a sense of maturity and clear goals, showing that the person has gone through a careful thought process based on past experiences and knowledge about future opportunities.

We admit people from many different work backgrounds. While work experience does not require a title of "Manager," there should be signs of progression in a person's responsibilities that provide exposure to managerial decision-making in different areas of the organization. All organizations require good management to remain successful, whether it be in the traditional corporate environment, a nonprofit organization, the military, or the theater.

When picking recommenders, choose those who can answer the questions on the school's recommendation form and who know you well. While a letter from a professor is allowed for those who have recently graduated, given the emphasis on work experience by our school, letters from work colleagues are preferred, and such people are usually better able to answer all of the questions on the form. Letters can come from supervisors, peers, vendors, or clients. A letter from a relative or from a high-level executive who does not know the applicant well is less impressive.

An undergraduate degree in business carries no more weight than another undergraduate degree. What is important is the type of work experience, levels of responsibility, and whether the applicant's future career goals make sense given these past experiences.

Applying early is most advantageous for those applicants who feel they may qualify for a scholarship/fellowship based on academic merit and work experience. In general, there are still spots available for the final deadline, but most likely very few scholarships, if any.

Applying early is most advantageous for those applicants who feel they may qualify for a scholarship/ fellowship based on academic merit and work experience. In general, there are still spots available for the final deadline, but most likely very few scholarships, if any.

The time between thinking about pursuing an M.B.A. degree and actually meeting a deadline can take up to a year. The applicant should make sure to allow for plenty of time to study for the GMAT (a minimum of two to three months) and to ensure that prerequisite classes are fulfilled. If the applicant is unfamiliar with the school and its location, arranging a visit to the school, meeting current students, and possibly visiting a class could really help in the final decision-making process. No matter which program is chosen, it is a large investment of time and money, and an applicant should feel comfortable and confident about the final decision.

▶**Eleanor Polster**
College of Business Graduate Coordinator
Florida International University

Fast Facts about the Business School

Location: Miami, Florida

Enrollment: 820 (656 full-time, 164 part-time)

Degrees offered: Master of Business Administration (M.B.A.), Master of Science (M.S.) in finance, Master of Accountancy (M.Acc.), Executive M.B.A. (E.M.B.A.), Master of Science in Taxation (M.S.T.), Executive Master of Science in Taxation (E.M.S.T.)

Average age: 28

Web site: www.fiu.edu/~cba

In general, the best time for prospective students to start thinking about business school is one to two years after graduating from college. After a few years in the job market, students can bring their more practical knowledge of business problems to the classroom setting.

In today's business environment, it's important to continually update your knowledge in order to keep up with changes in the business environment. An advanced degree helps you learn how to think about business problems and how to put them in their proper perspective.

When choosing programs, prospective students should look at the schools' areas of expertise and whether or not they match their career objectives. Students should also consider the reputation of the school and the faculty. If a student can't move geographically or is constrained by monetary concerns, he or she should look at schools in the area that have the best reputation.

When reviewing a prospective application, in order of importance, Florida International University looks at the applicant's GMAT score, undergraduate GPA, letters of recommendation, work experience, and essays. We actually prefer students whose undergraduate degree is in a field other than business, although with comparable grades and test scores, we make no differentiation between various degrees when it comes to whether or not to accept a student. If someone's degree is not in business, we recommend that they have a

> **When choosing programs, prospective students should look at the schools' areas of expertise and whether or not they match their career objectives. Students should also consider the reputation of the school and the faculty.**

good quantitative and computer background. The school does not emphasize business work experience over other kinds of work experience, but we do prefer that applicants have work experience of some sort.

We ask students to write only one essay that explains why the student wants to get a business degree. In evaluating the essay, we look for good writing skills and indication of a genuine desire to obtain the degree.

When choosing recommenders, it's a good idea for students to ask their professors and people who know them in a business connection. Applicants should make sure the person knows them well enough to give a detailed description of why they would be a good student.

Timing makes no difference in our admission process. If we feel that someone will make a good student, we will admit them whether they apply early or late.

My advice? As you enter your quest for an advanced degree in business, be prepared for a rigorous but rewarding experience. You will be a better manager for the experience.

▶**James Stevens**
Director of Admissions
Yale School of Management

Fast Facts about the Business School

Location: New Haven, Connecticut
Enrollment: 432 (432 full-time, 0 part-time)
Degrees offered: M.B.A.
Average age: 27.5
Web site: www.yale.edu/som

(Note to the reader: With Mr. Stevens's review and approval, portions of his statement were culled from the Yale School of Management's Web site, www.yale.edu/som, and from a recent interview that you can access on line at www.businessweek.com.)

In today's increasingly competitive economy, the value of an advanced management degree is more apparent than ever. Whether an individual plans to work in a business, government, or nonprofit setting, the education acquired at a top M.B.A. program will serve him or her in countless ways. Practical skills in areas such as strategy, finance, marketing, operations, and economics form the foundation of a solid management education. However, learning how to think creatively in many situations, as well as how to apply these skills when faced with new challenges, demonstrates the true value of an excellent management education.

No time is too early for prospective business students to start collecting information about programs. At least a year in advance, they should start thinking about how an M.B.A. will fit their career goals, collecting information, and considering whom to ask for recommendations. Some people may need more time to plan than others and to retake the GMAT if necessary, so applicants should give themselves as much time as possible to allow for anything that may come up along the way.

The Yale School of Management (SOM) seeks to enroll students who demonstrate academic potential, professional accomplishment, leadership qualities, entrepreneurial skills, and certain personal qualities, such as high values and passion for the field. No single element of the application, therefore, would preclude an applicant from being considered for admission to the program. When we look at the GMAT, we consider the verbal, quantitative, and analytical writing assessment scores individually, but we also consider the applicant's overall score. Most of the students who enroll in the Yale M.B.A. program have at least two years of work experience, although on rare occasions we will accept someone with less than two years of experience. It's important for applicants to remember when they look at our average scores and years of working experience that these are just averages; some students fall above and some fall below these *averages*, so a prospective applicant should not be discouraged from applying to the program if his or her scores don't quite "match up" with our averages.

When we review the materials an applicant has submitted, we look at each prospective student as an *individual*. We take an overall view of the applicant to determine what he or she will gain from and contribute to the program and whether we would be proud to have him or her as a graduate of the Yale School of Management. Several members of the admissions committee review each application, and then we discuss each applicant as a group before making our decision. By the time we offer someone a spot in the program, we know him or her very well.

What do we look for in particular when we review a student's application? We like to see that the student is realistic about his or her goals and that these goals fit with what the school can do to meet them. Because our program is very collaborative and our students work together on teams and play an active role in setting the direction of Yale SOM, we look for people whom we believe will be involved and will work well together. We look for applicants who will benefit from the school's mission to educate leaders for business and society; we want to enroll men and women who will make an impact wherever they go. We place a lot of emphasis on finding students with strong communication skills—this is essential for admission to the program. Of course, no single criterion will be able to tell us all of this, so we look at every element of the application to get a real sense of the individual.

The Yale School of Management requires three recommendations. We believe that it's important to get as broad a perspective about an applicant as we can. We ask for one academic recommendation, unless

It's important for applicants to remember when they look at our average scores and years of working experience that these are just averages; some students fall above and some fall below these averages, so a prospective applicant should not be discouraged from applying to the program if his or her scores don't quite "match up" with our averages.

the student has been out of school for quite a while, and two professional recommendations. Believe it or not, we've seen people submit recommendations from their parents, their best friend, or their brother-in-law. Needless to say, this is a mistake, as it raises questions about the applicant's judgment. Each recommender should offer a different perspective on the applicant and his or her work. If the applicant has worked for more than one employer, we like to see recommendations from the current employer as well as a previous employer. This, we hope, will show an applicant's growth from position to position. If you're an entrepreneur, I'd recommend that you turn to your colleagues, suppliers, and especially your clients, all of whom can give is a sense of your professional abilities.

Most of our currently enrolled students do not come from undergraduate majors in business-related fields. Business administration and economics majors make up only 35 percent of our students; humanities/liberal arts majors comprise over 20 percent of the student body, engineering majors almost 15 percent, science/math majors a little over 12 percent, and those from other social sciences about 17 percent. An applicant's undergraduate major isn't as important to us. However, several of our first-year core courses involve rigorous quantitative methods, and the quantitative ability of all applicants is carefully evaluated. Complete proficiency in algebra is expected of all incoming students. Prospective students are therefore strongly advised to enroll in courses in college-level calculus, statistics, and microeconomics prior to or while applying.

Yale's application process consists of three separate rounds of deadlines, and we send out decisions for each admissions round as a group. In general, we tend to see stronger applicants in the first round, but which round you apply for doesn't really make any difference, since an individual applicant's chance of admission is about the same in all three rounds. In some cases, we will defer a decision on a candidate until the next round to compare him or her to the remaining applicant pool.

Some words of advice? When applying, I don't think it's a good idea for students to apply to only one "dream" school. In general, you should apply to one or two dream schools, one or two schools that are a good fit for you and where you're confident you'll be accepted, and one or two schools that are a sure thing. With the increased application competitiveness that we're seeing these days, you should make sure that you have several options at the end of the application cycle.

▶**Pamela Van Epps, Ph.D.**
Coordinator of Graduate Programs
College of Business Administration
Loyola University New Orleans

Fast Facts about the Business School

Location: New Orleans, Louisiana

Enrollment: 83 (28 full-time, 55 part-time)

Degrees offered: Master of Business Administration (M.B.A.), Master of Quality Management (M.Q.M.), joint M.B.A./Doctor of Jurisprudence (J.D.)

Average age: 35

Web site: www.cba.loyno.edu

Don't ask a relative or best friend to make a recommendation. The best recommendations come from academic and/or professional references who are willing to take the time to personalize a recommendation.

Loyola University New Orleans does not require work experience; however, it is strongly recommended. For those who don't have much or any significant work experience, our admissions committee will look at the resume very closely for evidence of internships, leadership roles in student organizations, school work-study positions, summer jobs, and so on. This is also a good topic to address in the essay, if the opportunity is available.

Regarding recommendations, I strongly advise that you don't ask a relative or best friend to make the recommendation. The best recommendations come from academic and/or professional references who are willing to take the time to personalize a recommendation as opposed to sending a "canned" one.

For admission to Loyola New Orleans, there is no undergraduate degree that is more advantageous than another; however, students who have graduated within seven years of M.B.A. admission with a undergraduate business degree from a school accredited by the International Association for Management Education (AACSB) are permitted to waive foundation courses in which they earned a B or better (many excellent schools offer this or a similar waiver policy.) Prospective M.B.A. students with undergraduate business degrees seeking to shorten their studies would be wise to look for AACSB-accredited M.B.A. programs that offer such an option.

Advice from Business School Students

In this book, we've given you some practical advice that we hope will help you choose and get admitted to the business program that's right for you. We've also had admissions personnel weigh in on what they feel you can do to pick the perfect program and make your application stand out from the crowd. But really, who knows better about business school than the students themselves? This chapter lets business school students speak for themselves—about why they decided to get a graduate degree in business, how long they waited before going to graduate school and why, how hard they found the application process, what their employers did for them along the way, and what they think a business degree will do for them.

The eleven students profiled here responded to an e-mail questionnaire comprising the following questions:

- What made you decide to get a graduate degree in a business field? Were you looking to change careers or enhance the career you had? Do most others in your field have graduate degrees in business?
- Did you go on to graduate school immediately after undergraduate school, or did you wait? If you waited, how long before you went back? Do you think you made the right choice in waiting or not waiting?
- If your undergraduate degree was not in business, did you have to take any classes to make up differences before you moved on to graduate studies?
- If you're going for an M.B.A., what made you choose that degree over an M.S. or M.A. degree in a business field? What do you feel is the advantage of the M.B.A. degree?

- If you're going for an M.S. or M.A. degree in a business-related field, why did you decide to go for that over an M.B.A.? What do you feel is the advantage of the M.S. degree?
- How hard was it to get into the program to which you applied?
- What part did your employer play (if any) in your decision to get an advanced degree? Were you encouraged by them to do so? Did they pay for all or part of your degree? What accommodations did they make for you while you went back for your degree?
- Did you take the GMAT? Was it necessary for your program? How hard did you find the test?
- What do you think your degree in business will do for you? Do you think it will give you an edge over others without this degree?
- Finally, what words of wisdom would you impart to others who are thinking of going to business school, especially regarding the application and admission process?

In compiling this chapter, respondents' answers to these questions were edited only insomuch as it was necessary to have them flow in paragraph form. We have used just the students' first names to preserve their anonymity.

▶Andrew

Age: 27
Current job title: Senior Auditor/Consultant, Ernst & Young LLP
Undergraduate degree: Accountancy
Working toward: M.B.A., with a concentration in finance

I decided to go for a graduate degree in business to increase and broaden my knowledge and continue to be successful in my current career path; I am looking to enhance the career I already have. Most others in my field do not have a graduate degree in business.

I waited four years after getting my undergraduate degree to begin graduate studies. I think it was a good choice to wait at least two years, but I'm glad that I didn't wait more than four years. In my opinion, two years of work experience before returning to graduate school is necessary to gain enough knowledge of the professional working environment and certain business issues, such as transactions and industry roles.

My employer, Ernst & Young (E&Y), notifies employees of opportunities to seek corporate sponsorship to pay for business school. The specific people I worked with encouraged me to apply for sponsorship. I am enrolled in their Summer M.B.A. Program, where I take classes full-time in three consecutive summers and attend one or two classes in the intervening fall and spring semesters. This arrangement is worked out between the program and my employer. E&Y is paying all costs related to the program.

It was necessary for me to take the GMAT for admission to the program I'm in. I found it equivalent in difficulty to the SAT in terms of performance. In terms of actual difficulty, the GMAT is a little harder, but not much. The sections of the GMAT that aren't on the SAT are a little more difficult.

Getting an M.B.A. will certainly make me a more well-rounded business professional. I will have a better understanding of more complex, advanced financial concepts, theories, and models and will better understand the roles of different players in the industry. Although getting the degree won't *directly* help me advance within the company, it will help me be better at my job, which will *indirectly* help me advance quicker. If I decide to go elsewhere, having an M.B.A. will definitely give me an edge over others.

Words of advice: I only applied to one business school, so the application and admission process was not too involved for me. I would suggest that applicants try to find a few schools that they might enjoy and benefit from attending, be realistic about their chances of being accepted, and not fill out applications for a ton of schools.

▶Beau

Age: 35
Not currently employed
Undergraduate degrees: Philosophy and economics
Working toward: M.B.A.

The impetus for me to go back for a degree in business was because I'm looking to change from a career with the government to one in the private sector. I waited a long time to return to business school, more than ten years. I think the right age to return is probably closer to 27 or

> **In my opinion, two years of work experience before returning to graduate school is necessary to gain enough knowledge of the professional working environment and certain business issues, such as transactions and industry roles.**

Game Plan for Getting into Business School

29, but I was married at that time and had other things going on in my life. My wife and I decided that she should finish law school before I returned for a graduate degree. I decided to pursue an M.B.A. over other business-related degrees because I think it will make me more marketable.

It was necessary to take the GMAT to get admitted to the program I'm in. I found the GMAT hard but not impossible, and I would recommend taking a GMAT review course if you've been out of school for a while. What was even more difficult, though, was getting admitted to the program itself. The acceptance rate is 11 percent overall, and I really think it's harder to get admitted if you're older than 32.

Words of advice: M.B.A. applicants who are older than 30 need to be prepared to have a rougher time getting in. You have to have a good story that makes sense, and you need to know where you're going. Be prepared to be rejected. Reapply and prove you're serious.

> **I found the GMAT hard but not impossible, and I would recommend taking a GMAT review course if you've been out of school for a while.**

▶Cynthia

Age: 33
Current job title: Project Manager, E-Commerce Division, Providian
Undergraduate degree: Sociology/anthropology
Working toward: Master of Science (M.S.) in human resources
   management

I currently work in the "business world" and could not, at this time, dramatically change careers. So I decided to take advantage of the best of both worlds. I decided on HR management because it gives me an outlet to keep in touch and work with people while still maintaining a foothold in business. I would say that I am looking to enhance the career that I already have in the short term and to change careers in the long term. In my present field, most people do not have advanced degrees in business.

I waited ten years before returning for a graduate degree. I'm not sure if I made the right choice by waiting this long, but because I'm older, I'm very focused on what I'm learning, and my business experience has given me a great base. I'm not sure I would have completed this degree if I had decided to attend graduate school directly out of college.

I decided to get an M.S. over an M.B.A. because I wasn't really interested in the broader picture that an M.B.A. provides. At this time in my life, I'd rather focus on what I like to do or see myself doing in the future. For someone in this position, I think that a specialized M.S. or M.A. degree is better than an M.B.A. degree. To get into the graduate program, I had to apply, write an essay, and submit a transcript of my undergraduate grades and classes. I was conditionally admitted and had to maintain a particular grade point average through three classes—which I did, so I'm now fully admitted to the program. I only had to take two undergraduate classes to fill in "gaps"—small computers in business and an undergraduate human resources management class. I did not have to take the GMAT.

I think that an advanced degree in business will allow me to move within my organization and will give me a little more freedom to apply for positions that I may not necessarily qualify for at this time. I think a graduate degree will definitely give me an edge over others without one.

Words of advice: Don't be discouraged if you have an undergraduate degree in a field that's not business-related. When considering graduate programs, think about what you're interested in, what your real-world job and education experiences are, and what your long-term goals are. Don't look only at how much money you'll make when you get your degree. You should find a program that complements the experiences and interests you have and go from there.

▶Gary

Age: 27
Current job title: Manager (Audit Practice), Ernst & Young LLP
Undergraduate degree: Accounting
Working toward: M.B.A.

I decided to get a graduate degree in business because I wanted to get a "bigger picture" of the business world and to broaden my options in the business world. I am looking to enhance my current career but also to develop skills that will give me the opportunity to change careers should I ever decide to do so. Most others in my field do not have graduate degrees in business.

> **At this time in my life, I'd rather focus on what I like to do or see myself doing in the future. For someone in this position, I think that a specialized M.S. or M.A. degree is better than an M.B.A. degree.**

I waited four years after getting my undergraduate degree before returning to graduate school. I think that was definitely the right decision. Not only is it hard to get into a good business program right after undergraduate school, but I also think that it makes the experience more worthwhile when you come into graduate school with previous work experience. I'm working toward an M.B.A. as opposed to a specialized M.S. or M.A. degree because I think the M.B.A. gives you the ability to move around in the business world much more easily than a specialized degree does. I also think that an M.B.A. gives you better tools to manage others effectively.

My employer played some part in my decision to get an advanced degree, but I always knew I wanted to get an M.B.A. eventually. E&Y allows me to attend a full semester of classes over the summers (with minimal work responsibilities) and to take one or two classes during the other semesters while working. They also offer several other programs for returning for an advanced business degree. E&Y is paying for all of the expenses I incur.

Words of advice: Those who are thinking about going to business school should look into the programs each school offers, as some schools specialize in certain fields (e.g., marketing, finance, or economics) in which they may have an interest. Also, prospective students should have some idea before they enter a program about what they want to do with their degree upon graduation, especially if they are going back full-time. I think applicants should also speak to people who have already gone or are in the process of going to business school at the time they are considering applying in order to have more insight into various programs.

▶Iraj

Age not reported
Current job title: Financial Analyst, Federal Reserve Bank of New York
Undergraduate degree: Economics
Working toward: M.B.A.

I decided to return for an M.B.A. to further myself in the job I already have; I was looking to enhance my career. I chose to return for an M.B.A. rather than a specialized M.S. or M.A. degree because I want a

> **I'm working toward an M.B.A. as opposed to a specialized M.S. or M.A. degree because I think the M.B.A. gives you the ability to move around in the business world much more easily than a specialized degree does. I also think that an M.B.A. giver you better tools to manage others effectively.**

well-rounded course of business study and I wasn't exactly sure of my concentration. Most others in my field do have graduate degrees in business. Having an M.B.A. degree will definitely be an advantage; it will increase my chances of reaching more senior-level positions at my job. I waited three years after I received my undergraduate degree before I returned to graduate school. It was definitely worth waiting.

It was very difficult to get into the graduate program, but I found the GMAT to be relatively easy. I had to take several basic accounting and finance classes before I began the program. My employer is sponsoring me (i.e., paying for the program), but they did not encourage me to attend. It was strictly my ambition to get an M.B.A. My employer lets me miss work to attend class.

Words of advice: Don't be afraid to be "different" and/or creative in filling out your business school application. Feel free to emphasize unusual or extraordinary events in your life, not just the business-related ones.

▶Karen

Age: 27
Current job title: Manager, Deloitte & Touche LLP
Undergraduate degree: Accounting
Working toward: M.B.A.

I decided to go back to graduate school because I was looking for a change; I wanted to take classes in international business and finance since I was planning to go overseas to work, and I wanted to enhance my knowledge base. I am looking to enhance my current career. Some in my field have graduate degrees in business, but it's not a requirement. I waited four years before I went back to graduate school. I think this was the right choice, since I am now in a position to utilize some of the information I have learned.

To get into the program, I had to apply through my job first, since I'm a corporate-sponsored student. My employer was instrumental in my decision to go back for a graduate degree. As I said before, it's not required for my position, but it is one of the many opportunities the company offers its employees. Deloitte & Touche pays for the entire program, and I have a two-year commitment to them after the program.

> **Having an M.B.A. degree will definitely be an advantage; it will increase my chances of reaching more senior-level positions at my job.**

> **I waited four
> years before I
> went back to
> graduate school. I
> think this was the
> right choice, since
> I am now in a
> position to utilize
> some of the
> information I
> have learned.**

I had to take the GMAT for admission to the business program, and I found it very much like the SAT. I took the test two years out of undergraduate school and very soon after I took and passed the CPA exam, so I was still used to taking standardized tests.

I think that an advanced degree will provide me with more information about the financial realm; since I currently do not have an understanding of this market, I've taken some courses to fill this gap. I hope the degree will give me an edge over others without it. Eventually, I would like to move more into a consulting-type role and to work on transactions for clients. I am currently on the audit side of the company and would like to do other things in the firm.

Words of advice: I would suggest that you get to know the people you are in school with. This is a great opportunity to meet new people. Sure, you are making good contacts and networking, but more importantly, you have an opportunity to make some good friends. This is probably the last time you will be in school, so it is worth making the most of it. I would also suggest not focusing on grades so much but on the learning experience both in and out of the classroom. Above all, have fun!

►Margaret

Age: 28
Current job title: Manager, Ernst & Young LLP
Undergraduate degree: Accounting
Working toward: M.B.A.

When I learned that my firm offered a program at Columbia University, I was thrilled at having the opportunity to obtain my M.B.A. without having to pay for the degree or give up my salary for a traditional two-year program. Most people in my field do not have an M.B.A., but it is becoming more common. I graduated from Georgetown University in 1993 and started the Columbia program in 1997. I can't imagine going straight to business school from undergraduate school, since so much of the classroom discussions draw upon your work experience.

The partners for whom I work supported me in my decision to obtain an M.B.A. The program I participated in, known as the Summer

MBA Program, required full-time attendance for three summers, with the remaining five classes being attended during the semesters in between. The people I work for definitely had to accommodate me. Getting into the program was competitive, but I didn't find the GMAT to be very hard at all. It requires that you work quickly through problems under given time constraints, but the material did not seem very difficult.

I feel that the degree will definitely give me an edge over others. It will help me both through the business contacts that I made while in the program and through the insight I gained into serving my clients. Only time will tell—I just graduated!

Words of advice: Start early, and really put care into what you say in your essays—they are the best reflection of "you" to the admissions committee. Also, the recommendations are key, so pick those individuals carefully.

▶P. K.

Age not reported
Current job title: Managing Director, CEMCOM Corp.
Undergraduate degree: Mathematics
Graduate degree: M.S. in industrial and management engineering
Working toward: M.B.A.

I decided to go to business school for an M.B.A. to learn financial skills. At the time I applied to business school, I was looking to enhance my skills, but now I am looking to change careers. It's been sixteen years since I received my undergraduate degree. For me, it wasn't a choice to wait this long; it's just the way my life worked out. I chose to get an M.B.A. at the best business school I could get into. Getting an M.B.A. from a "top ten" business school was best for me.

It was extremely hard to get into the business program I'm enrolled in. I was on the wait list and couldn't seem to get off. I reapplied for the January term and was finally accepted for the May class. To get admitted to the program, I had to take some marketing courses and a finance course at night. I had to take the GMAT for admission; I found the grammar section to be very difficult, but the rest was not too hard.

I graduated from Georgetown University in 1993 and started the Columbia program in 1997. I can't imagine going straight to business school from undergraduate school, since so much of the classroom discussions draw upon your work experience.

Going for my business degree has given me tremendous self-confidence. I have learned financial skills and have established a great network. It has opened up a whole bunch of career opportunities for me. An M.B.A. degree is a signal; it informs potential employers that I am a pretty smart individual with business skills.

Words of advice: Apply early—in the fall. Do not wait until after the first of the year.

▶Rosina

Age not reported
Not currently employed
Undergraduate degree: Accounting
Working toward: M.B.A.

I have always had a personal goal to get an advanced degree. I chose business over law because I found that a business degree, particularly from a top institution, would provide me with infinite opportunities that I would not otherwise have. I am getting my degree to change careers. My interpretation of the difference between an M.S. in a business area and an M.B.A. is that an M.S. is much more theoretical in content and is geared to academics, versus an M.B.A., which focuses more on the application of the theory to various business situations. An M.B.A. also offers a more comprehensive education, as it touches upon the interrelationship between the various disciplines in business.

I waited four years after completing undergraduate school to go on to graduate school. I strongly believe that it was the right choice to wait. The ability to apply past experiences to current business situations is a key advantage in business school. I feel that I get so much more out of classes because I am able to relate to the information being presented.

I had to take the GMAT for admission to the program. The hardest part about the test is remembering basic level math problems. The key to the GMAT is practice, practice, practice. It's difficult for me to say how hard it was to get into the program; here I am at Harvard Business School, and I sometimes wonder how I got in!

I feel that an M.B.A., particularly from Harvard, will give me access to a vast network of alumni as well as current students who are ready to provide advice and open doors to various career paths. In

Going for my business degree has given me tremendous self-confidence. . . . An M.B.A. degree is a signal; it informs potential employers that I am a pretty smart individual with business skills.

addition, the education itself has provided me with an opportunity to listen to and meet great businesspeople who have transformed and continue to shape the business world.

Words of advice: The first day of my GMAT review program, I was told that this was the most important exam I would ever take, as it would determine the rest of my life. I absolutely disagree with this statement. Although it is an important element of the admissions process, do not stress too much about it. The more you stress, the worse you will do.

▶Susan

Age: 29
Current job title: Assistant Product Director, Johnson & Johnson
Undergraduate degree: Psychology
Working toward: M.B.A.

I decided to get an advanced degree in business because the business world offers more opportunities than a career in law, which was my first career choice. When I enrolled in the program, I was looking to change careers. Most others in my field have graduate degrees in business. I waited five years after getting my undergraduate degree to go to graduate school. I wish I hadn't waited that long.

I chose an M.B.A. over a specialized M.S. degree because I wanted to get a broad set of business skills. I feel that the M.B.A. degree creates well-rounded business managers and allows for future career changes. I feel that having an M.B.A. will give me credibility and will, without a doubt, give me an edge over others without this degree. It has tripled my earning potential already!

Getting into the program was very competitive; I think that my interview tipped the scales in my favor. To strengthen my quantitative skills, I took an accounting class at a community college before applying to the program. I had to take the GMAT for admission, but I didn't find it that hard. The GMAT is a skills-based test, and you can work at improving those skills if you need to.

Words of advice: Don't be discouraged if you come from an unconventional professional background. If anything, it will work in your

> My interpretation of the difference between an M.S. in a business area and an M.B.A. is that an M.S. is much more theoretical in content and is geared to academics, versus an M.B.A., which focuses more on the application of the theory to various business situations.

favor! I did not come from Wall Street or consulting, but rather owned a dry cleaning business, which is certainly not the norm.

▶Vineet

Age: 27
Current job title: Vice President, Chase Manhattan Bank
Undergraduate degree: Mechanical engineering
Working toward: M.B.A.

I decided to get a graduate degree in business because of the lack of advancement opportunities in my field. When I enrolled in the program, I was looking to change careers. Most others in my field have graduate degrees in business. I feel that getting an advanced degree in business will give me more experiences to rely on in the business world. I will undoubtedly have an edge over others without the degree.

I waited four years before I returned to school for my graduate degree, and I think it was an excellent choice to wait. Having four or five years of solid preparation for post-undergraduate school is crucial in order for someone to get the most out of the program.

It was quite difficult to get into the business program, but I found the GMAT to be extremely easy. I didn't have to take any extra courses before enrolling, even though my undergraduate degree was not in a business field. My employer paid for my business degree and was very accommodating after finding out that my intent was to return to school full-time.

Words of advice: Make sure to find a school with a curriculum that fits your interests; don't just go to the biggest name school you can find. Also, looking at job placement information from prospective schools is important so you can evaluate whether or not the schools have links to the businesses/industries you are considering for employment after graduation.

> I feel that having an M.B.A. will give me credibility and will, without a doubt, give me an edge over others without this degree. It has tripled my earnng potential already!

Studying Abroad for Your Business Degree

Chapter 8

If you've ever thought about studying in another country, doing so for a business degree may be a great idea. These days, students seeking careers in business are realizing the value of international study. Studying abroad is one of the most effective ways to obtain knowledge and develop skills that will help you succeed in the global context of today's business world. The traits that employers will value highly in the twenty-first century—cross-cultural sensitivity, international mobility, and foreign language proficiency—can be gained from getting your business degree abroad.

Why is international experience becoming more highly valued in today's job marketplace? To begin with, think of the scores of transnational companies whose operations—and business-related jobs—have spread across numerous countries. The rapid growth of communications technology, which enables employees of the same company to communicate easily from any point on the globe, also means that companies can now take advantage of emerging business opportunities in markets that formerly were closed to them. Companies with a global perspective are eager to develop joint ventures and start-up operations in these markets, but without skilled personnel who can manage in different cultural and linguistic contexts, such business opportunities may go to waste.

That's where you come in. Demand for business majors with foreign language skills and cross-cultural knowledge is high. With a business degree from a college or university in another country, you'll be able to apply for jobs in exotic ports of call-and get them. If you've dreamed about studying and working in Italy, Hong Kong, Indonesia, or Japan, now's your chance. Opportunities for studying and working abroad have never been better. All you have to do is choose the program that best serves your goals. And that, of course, is what we're here for.

MAKING THE DECISION TO GET YOUR BUSINESS DEGREE ABROAD

How can you tell if studying abroad for your business degree is the best choice for you? As we'll discuss later on in this chapter, many fine programs throughout the United States offer business curriculums with an international dimension. Why, then, would you want or need to study in another country for your degree? If you've done some serious thinking about your career goals, maybe you've decided that an intensive experience abroad that incorporates foreign language and cultural skills would best help you reach these goals. Perhaps you've realized that building an international network of professional contacts would be a big advantage to your career. Or maybe, just a romantic at heart, you've always longed to travel and become a "citizen of the world." All of these are fine reasons to pursue business studies overseas.

Have you already had significant experiences abroad? If so, getting your degree at an overseas university could go one of two ways: You could find that studying in that country really doesn't add that much value to the experiences you've already had, which would not be the best use of your time, or you could find that studying abroad will help you build on skills you acquired in previous experiences, develop higher levels of language competence, and gain in-depth knowledge of the country or region where you'd like to study and work. Before you look into studying abroad, think about how much you really can gain from the experience. If you already spent two years in Japan as an undergraduate, is there much more to be learned from going to business school there? Only you can decide.

Studying abroad is an extremely *intense* experience, moreso if you've never studied outside the United States before. Given that your life as a business school student in and of itself will be incredibly demanding, you need to think long and hard about whether you'll be able to handle the extra responsibilities—or if you'll even need to. Talk to your colleagues and supervisors about what they feel the benefits of

According to the American Institute for Foreign Study (AIFS), more than 113,000 U.S. students chose to study abroad in 1997–98. That number is up *over 14.5%* from the year before.

getting your degree abroad may be. Is it necessary for the career track on which you'd like to embark? Traveling to another country to get an advanced degree is not something to be taken lightly. Chances are that you'll be plunged into a intensive language-learning environment; this will be in addition to your business studies, which will be grueling. Perhaps you could get the same advantages from taking a few language classes at home or enrolling in one of the United States–based international business programs that we'll discuss later in this chapter. If you decide that studying abroad is right for you, be prepared to be challenged.

And speaking of the language-learning environment, how up to snuff are your foreign language skills, anyway? Foreign language proficiency can be a defining criterion in deciding whether or not to study abroad. Although many programs in locations around the globe are offered in English, most require some level of proficiency in the language of the country. And of course, you'll need to communicate in order to *live* in the country in which you'll be studying. Imagine how frustrating ordering dinner—or taking public transportation, doing your laundry, or reading the newspaper—will be if you don't have the most basic knowledge of your host country's language. If the program offers or requires intensive language immersion, you'll benefit in the long run if your language skills aren't quite up to par in the beginning. Remember again, however, that learning the language will be in *addition* to learning the business curriculum. You may want to consider taking a refresher course—or a basic course if you have no language skills—before you enroll in a study-abroad program.

> AIFS reports that the United Kingdom is the top choice for students who study abroad. Spain, Italy, France, and Mexico round out the top five spots.

Finally, unless you have spent a lot of time in the country in which you plan to study, don't discount the "culture shock" factor. It is very likely that you will be affected in many, many ways by your reactions to living in another country. Depending on the culture in which you'll be immersed, you can expect lifestyle, values, and professional attitudes that are very different from your own. Will you be able to adapt? You won't be there to change your hosts' ways of thinking. You will need to accept and thrive in a foreign environment. This will not be an easy adjustment. But remember, acquiring the skills needed to work and learn in more than one culture is one of the reasons you wanted to study abroad in the first place. In the past, have you been open to new

Traveling to another country to get an advanced degree is not something to be taken lightly. Chances are that you'll be plunged into an intensive language-learning environment; this will be in addition to your business studies, which will be grueling.

experiences, and have you been accepting of those from other cultures? If so, all you will need is an open mind to be successful. If not, you should probably reconsider your choice to study abroad.

CHOOSING THE BEST PROGRAM FOR YOU

When looking at overseas programs, you'll need to think about all of the factors we discussed in Chapter 3—size, urban or rural location, faculty and program reputation, costs, campus culture, and so on—but you'll also need to pay attention to several things that are specific to studying abroad. First, consider where you may want to work after obtaining your degree. An obvious reason for choosing to study for a business degree abroad is to increase your chances of obtaining employment outside the United States. If you have your heart set on living or working in Italy or Japan, for instance, it makes sense to think about attending a program in that country. This is especially true if you'd like to work for a firm that is based in that country, not for a U.S. firm with a branch there. Studying in your country of choice has two benefits: First, the university from which you graduate will be recognized more easily by potential employers, and second, the program you attend will more than likely have placement services, alumni relations, and other ways of connecting graduates with the labor market in that country.

When considering programs in other countries, keep in mind that not all programs offer certain degrees. For instance, the M.B.A. degree is not offered as widely in other countries as it is in the United States. But other programs have fine advanced business and economics programs that, although the terminal degree is not the M.B.A., will make you competitive in that country's job market. If you feel that you may want to work in the United States at a later date, you'll need to look at the degrees being offered in overseas programs and how they translate into the U.S. job market.

You may also have to do some exploring to find a program that meets your language skills. If you're not fluent in the language of the country, don't enroll in a program taught exclusively in that language, unless a well-established intensive language-learning program is offered in conjunction with it. As we mentioned before, many programs around the world offer advanced business programs in English—in some countries moreso than in others—so you needn't let your foreign language skill set slow you down. You will, however, as we mentioned before, have to commit yourself to learning the language at some point, even if the program is offered in English. For some programs, foreign language requirements are often significant, even at schools that teach in English. Be sure to inform yourself about foreign language requirements before entering any program. If you need to prepare beforehand, be sure to do so.

It's important to find out about any overseas program's accreditation before you enroll. Some programs may be licensed by the city's department of commerce or industry as a *business*, but the degrees being offered may not be recognized by the country's university-level education authorities, usually the Ministry of Education. If a program is not recognized as *academically* legitimate in the country in which it operates, it is doubtful that its graduates have credibility in the international employment market. Find out whether the school—and the degree—are accredited by the Ministry of Education in the country where the school operates. The country's embassy or consulate can also provide useful information about the standing of the program.

With any business program, it's always useful to speak with some graduates, and this is especially true for overseas programs. Have the program provide you with the names of several U.S. graduates. Speak to them not only about the quality of their experiences and whether they felt graduating from the program was helpful in their careers but also about how students from other countries are treated in the program, whether they enjoyed living in the country, what the classes were like, and the level of language proficiency necessary to survive in the community. Before they enrolled in the graduate program, were their experiences similar to yours? In other words, had they traveled or studied abroad before? Did they have language proficiency? Also, find out about their undergraduate and working environments before they enrolled in the program. You want to talk to graduates whose experiences before the program are similar to yours so that you can best assess what you will be able to get out of the program.

> In Japan, the language barrier can be significant, since very few Japanese universities have programs targeted to international students that are taught in English. Combined with the Japanese tendency toward in-company education, this makes Japan an especially difficult area for international students to penetrate.

Questions to Ask If You're Thinking about Studying Abroad

Ask Yourself

- Why do I want to get my degree abroad? Do I want to eventually work in this country? Do I want to become more proficient in the language of the country? Do I want to establish international business contacts? Do I want to travel and see the world?

- What kind of setting would be best for me? A large or a small city? One whose culture is totally foreign or one whose culture incorporates more Western ways of life? One where English is spoken predominantly or one where English is spoken less so?

- How much challenge can I handle? Will I be able to adjust to a drastically different culture? Will I become homesick?

- What is my proficiency level in the language of this country? Is it good enough for the program? For the community in which I'll be living?

- While living there, do I want to live on campus or in town?

Ask the Program

- How academically sound is the program? Is it accredited? If so, by what organizations?

- What kinds of services does the program offer for American students?

- Does the program offer career placement opportunities? Where do graduates of the program get jobs?

- What is the breakdown of students by country? Will you be one of only a very few, or does the program serve many students from outside the country?

- What are the program's language requirements?

- What kind of orientation programs are offered for students coming from other countries?

- Will the program meet any special needs I have—physical and learning challenges, religious needs, or dietary requirements?

- Whom can I turn to if I run into problems while overseas? How are emergency situations and health issues handled?

- What kind of financial assistance can I get?

Taking the Jolt Out of Culture Shock

Before You Go

- Become very familiar with the new culture in which you'll be living. Find out about social issues, politics, customs, and history. Read up especially about any idiosyncrasies of the culture you are about to experience, and talk to others who have studied in or visited your host country. It may sound silly, but find out about the weather, too, and be prepared for it. Remember, a location that sounds like an island paradise may also have its share of tropical storms.

- Take advantage of predeparture and orientation materials sent to you by the program. If you're lucky, admissions personnel will offer lots of advice about how best to make your way in your new environment. Don't overlook any materials that they may send you, whether they're about local transportation, etiquette, or personal safety.

- Discuss practical information with people who've been to the country. Will your ATM card work? What about your hair dryer? What kind of clothing is appropriate? Where can you get your laundry done? What's the cheapest way to call home? It's best to know the answers to these and other daily-living questions before you find yourself in unfamiliar territory.

Once You're There

- Keep in touch with family and friends. E-mail is a great, inexpensive way to do this. Let everybody know what you're going through; not only will this help put the experience in perspective for you, but you'll also know that the people back home support you.

- Experience the culture! Don't stick with just the Americans. The key to learning about the culture is to make local friends. Visit museums, hang out in cafes, and enjoy local festivals. Go off the beaten path and really immerse yourself in the culture of the city, and you'll feel more comfortable. The more quickly you become familiar with your environs, the better you'll feel.

- Keep a journal while you're abroad. If you can't verbalize your impressions to friends and family, you may find it easier to write them down. In the years to come, you'll read and reread it and won't believe how much you grew from the experience.

FINANCING A BUSINESS PROGRAM OVERSEAS

The good news is that tuition for business programs overseas is rarely more than tuition for U.S. programs. But of course, just as some U.S. programs can run well into tens of thousands of dollars, so too can programs abroad. You'll also want to factor in the costs of airfare to and from the country in which you'll be studying. How often to you plan on returning to the states? A trip home for the winter holidays could run into thousands of dollars, especially if you're traveling from Eastern Europe or Australia, for example. Also, find out about the cost of living in the country and city in which you'll be living. It's well known that costs in Paris, Sydney, and other major cities rival those in New York City or San Francisco. If you can't afford to live in a metropolitan area in the United States, you definitely won't be able to afford to live in one abroad.

As we discussed in Chapter 5, many options exist to help you pay for a graduate degree in business. However, you may run into problems obtaining federally subsidized loans such as those that are available though U.S. college financial aid offices. Most of these loans have restrictions regarding the accreditation of institutions and programs and their eligibility for the loan program. Although some programs are more flexible in funding foreign study, you should check first about any regulations that may apply. Of course, most private loans won't have such restrictions, but those loans, as we discussed in Chapter 5, have higher interest rates than federal loans.

STUDYING AND LIVING ABROAD

Living and learning in another country demands adaptability, an adventurous spirit, and a willingness to adjust to life in another culture. Think of your study-abroad experience as both an opportunity and a challenge. Before you enroll in a study-abroad program, take the time to do some research on the country in which you will be living. Learn about its history, its religions, its geography, its mores, and its culture.

Decide whether or not this is someplace where you can feel comfortable for a few years (or more, should you decide to work there). The knowledge you acquire before you go will be invaluable as you adapt to a new country.

Before you go, be sure that you are prepared to handle the culture shock that you'll encounter once you arrive in your host country. Culture shock is different for everyone, but basically it's that feeling of unease that you have when you can't predict what's going to happen in any given situation. We can't tell you what your own culture shock will feel like, but rest assured that it will happen; if it doesn't, you're not getting anything out of the experience. While you're abroad, you'll go through many cycles of disorientation and accommodation, where you'll find yourself confronted with a new experience and will have to adapt to it to succeed. Recognize that this will happen to you, and commit yourself to go with the flow. One day you'll hate your host country; the next you'll be wondering how you could have lived anywhere else. This is the pattern of culture shock. If you accept beforehand that this crazy up-and-down feeling will be part of the overall study-abroad experience, you'll be better prepared to deal with the daily bouts of culture shock you'll inevitably face.

WHAT YOU'LL GAIN FROM A STUDY-ABROAD EXPERIENCE

You already know that studying abroad for your business degree will help you gain entry into the international job market. But what else can you expect to get out of studying abroad?

Those who have studied abroad talk about its many tangible and intangible benefits. Somehow, they emerge from their studies with experience and knowledge that go far beyond the course work that they've completed. Most say that studying abroad has influenced their lives in ways too numerous to count. For one, you discover that you can do things on your own in a land that definitely isn't your "home turf." You're thrown together with people who have a different way of looking at life, and somehow you survive. You grow, in other words, and gain a much larger view of the world and your place in it.

**Those who have
studied abroad
talk about its
many tangible
and intangible
benefits.
Somehow, they
emerge from their
studies with
experience and
knowledge that
go far beyond the
course work that
they've
completed.**

What you'll learn in the classroom will be just the beginning of your education. You'll have to tackle road signs in a foreign language, figure out how to order breakfast from a menu you can't read, and communicate with all the people who cross your path on a day-to-day basis. Perhaps this will be the first time that you'll truly be living independently. Even if you had your own apartment in the states, you could always count on your friends or your family to bail you out if the going got tough—or if the laundry piled up too high. Not so if you're abroad. Without this support system, you'll discover how strong you really are. You'll learn to handle difficult situations with ease and confidence, which will benefit you personally and in the workplace.

And those aren't the only skills that you'll develop that will have future employers lining up to hire you. Students who study abroad are known as risk-takers, as people willing to put themselves in unusual situations and make the most of them. An employer who sees a study-abroad experience on your resume will know that you're not afraid of the unknown and that it will take a lot to unnerve you. You'll be seen as a flexible go-getter, as someone who can adapt to new ways of thinking. And you'll have the perspective necessary to deal with clients and fellow workers from different cultures, a hot commodity in today's business environment.

Finally, leaving an environment that's familiar to you and embarking on an adventure of this magnitude have the potential to change your mind-set completely. You'll begin to see your place in the world and will come to understand how your U.S. citizenship factors into this. You've probably never thought about the fact that you're an "American," but there will be times when you'll be called upon to explain and even defend your country. Sometimes your newfound "outsider's" perspective will make you view American ways critically. In either case, you'll be forced to *think* about beliefs that you've probably taken for granted for a long time. In doing so, you'll learn a lot about yourself, the United States, and your place in it. That you are a citizen *of the world*, not just the United States, is perhaps the most life-altering realization that you will come to through a study-abroad experience.

FOR THE LESS ADVENTUROUS

Even after all we've talked about here, you may decide that getting a degree from an international university just isn't for you. Fortunately, you can gain global skills without leaving the United States by studying in one of the many U.S. programs that incorporate international experiences into their curricula. These less intensive options can't really be compared with living abroad, but you may find them preferable depending on your needs and aspirations. Peterson's *MBA Programs* includes information on a wealth of business programs that are offered in other countries, but you can also use this guide if you wish to research U.S. programs that have international dimensions built into the curricula. Several U.S. schools offer a master's degree in international business rather than a basic business degree; these programs, which include the Lauder Program at the University of Pennsylvania, a joint program of the Wharton School and the College of Arts and Science, require significant language and cultural knowledge. And an increasing number of programs, such as those offered by the University of Michigan, Indiana University, and San Diego State University, offer an international track or international fellows programs that require advanced foreign language competence and an overseas internship. Recognizing the priority that many employers are placing on global skills, many other U.S. business programs are now offering international internships and group projects outside the United States as a component of their curricula.

Several business schools offer joint-degree or double-degree options in conjunction with a business school in another country. The University of Texas at Austin (UT), for example, has several double-degree programs that allow students to get an M.B.A. from UT and, in one year abroad, obtain a degree from a French, German, or Mexican institution as well. A large number of M.B.A. students at New York University's Stern School take advantage of their extensive exchange programs with international business schools. Or you may want to look at schools where you can combine a business degree with a specialty in Asian or Eastern European studies.

If you're interested in incorporating an international element into your business school studies, you'll find no lack of programs to help you

> **Fortunately, you can gain global skills without leaving the United States by studying in one of the many U.S. programs that incorporate international experiences into their curricula.**

do so. Whether you choose a U.S. business program with an international element or an overseas business program should be a decision that you arrive at through a careful analysis of your experiences and your goals. In the end, you'll need to weigh the benefits of both options to determine what's the best course for you. If you decide to study abroad, we wish you "bonne chance" and hope that your journey is an enriching one.

Application Timeline

Keeping yourself organized throughout the information-gathering and application process is half the battle when it comes to getting admitted to business school. The best way to keep on track and stay sane during this hectic time is to (1) *start collecting information early* and (2) *have a set gameplan* that will take you all the way up to the day you send in your applications. Most admissions counselors advise that it takes at least one year to analyze your motives for returning to business school, investigate programs, gather information, take tests, request applications, and apply. With this in mind, we've provided you with a twelve-month countdown that takes you step-by-step through the admissions process. To make it easy, you may also want to photocopy our "Application Checklist" and fill it out for each program for which you've requested information. Remember, the most important part of applying is to keep track of the application procedure for each school.

Application Checklist
School name:
Date information requested:
Date information received:

Deadlines
     Application:
 	
     Financial aid:

Undergraduate transcripts requested:
Other transcripts requested (if applicable):
Undergraduate transcripts received:
Other transcripts received:
Letters of recommendation requested:
GMAT test date:
TOEFL test date (if applicable):
Essays written:

Appendix 1

Game Plan for Getting into Business School

Application Checklist
Resume updated:
Reminder to recommenders:
Fill out application form:
Gather recommendations:
Date application form sent:

Be sure to include:
Fee ____ Form ____ Recommendations ____ Essays ____
Transcripts ____ Resume ____

THE COUNTDOWN

Month Twelve

Think business school may be right for you? Now is the time to do some serious self-analysis before you begin collecting information about schools. Throughout month twelve, schedule an hour or so every other day—such short sessions will keep you from getting overwhelmed and will help you stay focused—to sit down and think carefully about why going back to school for an advanced degree in business may be right for you. Ask yourself these broad questions:

- Why do I want to go to business school? Do I think it will enhance my career, or am I looking for a career change?
- What experiences have I had that lead me to believe that business school is the best step for me at this point in my life?
- How interested am I in the field of business? Remember, it takes a lot of dedication to get through business school. You want to be sure you're doing it not just for financial gain or career advancement.
- Do I have the dedication, the time, and the energy to complete several years of advanced study?
- How does my family feel about my decision to attend business school?
- Will my employer support me in my decision to go to business school? Will I be able to have a more flexible schedule to accommodate increased demands, will I be able to scale back to part-time employment, and will my employer assume any of the financial responsibilities involved in graduate school?
- What is my overall financial situation? How will possibly having to take out several thousands of dollars in student loans affect this situation—both in the short run and in the long run?

The best way to keep on track and stay sane during this hectic time is to (1) *start collecting information early* and (2) *have a set gameplan* that will take you all the way up to the day you send in your applications.

You may want to keep a journal of your answers. As you review your responses to these questions, look for signs of a *desire and commitment* to go to business school. If your answers are lackluster (for example, "I guess it's just something I have to do if I want to succeed") and show that you're not wholeheartedly dedicated to returning to school, you probably want to reconsider taking the plunge at this point. By the same token, make sure that you have a strong support network in place before you go to graduate school; talk to family members about their opinion on this, and find out whether or not your employer will support and accommodate your decision. Examining your financial picture early on will also help you avoid "sticker shock" as you get further along in the process.

Month Eleven

Still interested in business school? Great! Now that you've done some broad thinking about returning to school, it's time to consider some specific questions. In month eleven, get those journals out and answer the following:

- Would it be better for me to attend business school full-time or part-time?
- What specific area of business studies am I most interested in?
- Am I willing to move to attend business school?
- Is the size of the school I attend important to me? What about the geographic location?
- Am I most comfortable learning in a teaching environment where there are a lot of lectures, or do I like working in teams on projects?

You may find it hard to think about such specific questions at this early stage, but believe us, focusing your search early is the best way to get admitted into the right program. You'll save a lot of time later on if you have pinpointed exactly what you want before you begin requesting information and applying.

Month Ten

In month ten, you'll begin investigating programs and requesting information from them. After spending the last two months doing some serious self-analysis, you should be able to identify those criteria that are most important to you. (You should also consult Chapter 3 in this book, which discusses different factors you may want to consider when looking at business programs.) Pick up a copy of Peterson's *MBA Programs* to begin your search. There you'll find information about over 900 institutions offering business programs around the world. For each program that piques your interest, visit their Web site and read more. If, based on your criteria, the program still sounds appealing to you, call or write to request more information—brochures, applications, and (especially) information about financial aid. When you receive information from programs, file each program separately, noting on the cover of the file the deadlines for both the application and financial aid. You may also want to take

Make sure that you have a strong support network in place before you go to graduate school; talk to family members about their opinion on this, and find out whether or not your employer will support and accommodate your decision.

a brief look through the application materials and note what's expected of you should you decide to apply—number of essays and recommendations, fee, resume, and so on.

Month Nine

Now that you've gathered all that information, it's time to go through it. Read each program's materials carefully. Look for all the points you've identified as being important to you. Remember, no matter how prestigious the program may be, it has to give you the opportunity to study the subjects you want. If you've decided to pursue a specialization in international business, for example, and the program doesn't offer it, take the program off your list. This is where your self-analysis will begin to pay off. By this time, you should be able to go through program materials fairly quickly and decide whether the program can give you what you want. If it can't, don't waste your time applying.

Once you narrow down your search to a few programs that may be right for you, call their admissions offices and schedule campus visits. Talk to your colleagues and your supervisors about their impression of the programs. Look more closely at the programs' financial aid options. Begin thinking about how much money you may need to borrow to attend the program.

Month Eight

In month eight, it's time to start preparing to take the GMAT. Begin by picking up a copy of Peterson's *GMAT Success*, which includes hundreds of practice questions, information about the GMAT-CAT, and "red alerts" that highlight key test-taking skills and strategies. The guide also includes Peterson's interactive GMAT test prep software, compatible to run on either Windows or Mac; the software features interactive practice questions, a diagnostic assessment of your skills, study tips and planning, and test scoring. The key to the GMAT is preparation and practice. If you think you may have a deficiency in one of the test areas, spend some time honing your skills. Take all of the practice tests. Consider enrolling in a GMAT prep course, but only if you're really not confident in your skills or if you think you may have problems taking standardized tests. Remember, everything they teach you in these courses you can learn on your own.

Finally, schedule an appointment to take the GMAT next month. With the advent of the GMAT-CAT, scheduling on short notice is no longer a hassle.

During this month you may also want to visit a few of the campuses in which you're interested. Refer back to Chapter 3 in this book before you make your visits. Make a list of questions about the school and the program that you'd like to ask admissions personnel, students, and faculty members. Be sure that you plan enough time during your visit to see the campus as a whole, the business school, and the surrounding town. When you return from your visits, take some time to think about your impressions of the school and the business program. Are you still interested in applying?

When you receive information from programs, file each program separately, noting on the cover of the file the deadlines for both the application and financial aid. You may also want to take a brief look through the application materials and note what's expected of you should you decide to apply.

Month Seven

D-Day: Time to take the GMAT. A few days before you take the test, visit the test site. Make sure you know where it is, how long it will take you to get there, and where you should park. This may sound simplistic, but the last thing you want to do on test day is get lost and be late for the test. Now that you've gathered information, visited some campuses, and narrowed down your list of schools, keep in mind which ones you'll be having your scores forwarded to. Remember, there will be an additional fee if you want your scores sent to more than four business schools.

The day before the test, make sure you get a good night's sleep. Eat well, and try not to stress out over the test too much. Keep in mind that you can take the test as many times as you like. On test day, eat a good breakfast to get your strength up. Wear comfortable clothes and shoes, and give yourself plenty of time to get to the test site. Take a deep breath, and good luck. You've prepared for this, so you should have no problems.

Month Six

Now that the GMAT is out of the way, it's time to turn to the applications themselves. Go back to the ones for the schools to which you'll be applying, and read through them carefully. What exactly is expected of you? One of the first things to look for is whether or not you'll need to take any courses to make up deficiencies on your transcripts. Remember, business schools look for students with excellent quantitative skills, so you may need to enroll in a review course in calculus or statistics to gain admission to the program. The best way to find out is to contact the program itself. Talk a little about your transcripts with admissions personnel; they'll be able to advise you about what you can and should do to ensure that you have the right academic qualifications.

At this point you should also start investigating scholarships and other sources of financial aid outside of those that may be available through the business school. Begin by reviewing Chapter 5 in this book and by picking up Patricia McWade's *Financing Graduate School* (Princeton, NJ: Peterson's, 1996) and Peterson's *Grants for Graduate & Postdoctoral Study*. Other sources of aid are also listed in Appendix II of this book. Be sure that you explore all of your financing options before taking out a loan.

Month Five

We know, you've been dreading it all along, but month five is the time for you to start working on those admissions essays. As we discussed in Chapter 4 and as many admissions directors in Chapter 6 noted, your essays are one of the most important elements of your application—sometimes, they're the most important element. You want to prepare a separate essay for each questions you're being asked by each and every school. Remember, admissions directors will know instinctively if your essay is a "canned" one that you've sent to many schools. Do yourself a favor and prepare each essay separately. Review the section in Chapter 4 about essays before you begin. If you spent months twelve

The key to the GMAT is preparation and practice. If you think you may have a deficiency in one of the test areas, spend some time honing your skills.

and eleven doing an in-depth self-analysis, you should be able to articulate why you want to go to business school and what you feel you can contribute to the programs. Now it's time to get it down on paper. In month five, start brainstorming about each of the questions. Make an outline discussing the points you'd like to address. In the months that follow, go back to the essays and refine them little by little.

In this month you'll also want to make sure that your resume and CV are up to date. Even if you're not required to submit a resume or CV to the programs to which you're applying, you'll want to be able to make them available to your recommenders (see Month Four). This way they'll have your work history and accomplishments in front of them as they prepare their letters. When updating your resume, be sure to include all of your accolades (e.g., published papers, lectures, professional awards), memberships in professional organizations, and leadership positions both in the workplace and in extracurricular pursuits.

> **Remember, admissions directors will know instinctively if your essay is a "canned" one that you've sent out to a bunch of schools. Do yourself a favor and prepare each essay separately.**

Month Four

In month four, approach the people that you've decided should write your recommendations. Refer back to the section on recommendations in Chapter 4 before you do so. As several of the admissions directors pointed out in Chapter 6, be sure that the people you ask to write your recommendations can speak about your academic qualifications or, preferably, your work experience. If choosing recommenders from your workplace, be sure to ask someone that can speak specifically about the job you have done and how you have progressed in your career. Having the CEO to write a recommendation will not impress admissions committees if he or she can't speak directly to your experience on the job. If you've had more than one job, ask someone from each workplace to write a recommendation. If there are gaps in your resume or transcript, have one of your recommenders address those gaps. Make sure that the recommenders you choose really have the time to put into this project. If someone you approach seems hesitant, ask someone else. Tell the recommenders when you'll be collecting their letters, and supply them with labeled envelopes and a copy of your resume.

Month Three

In month three, contact your undergraduate school for a copy of your transcripts. If you've attended any other institutions of higher learning, even if only for a class of two, you'll need to get transcripts from them, too. You'll probably have to pay for a copy of your transcripts. When you receive your transcripts, review them carefully for any mistakes. Report errors immediately to the school, and have them rectified before you submit your transcripts to the business programs. Photocopy several copies of your transcripts.

Are you still working on your essays? Remember, you should be taking time each month to polish them. At this stage, you should be ready to have other people look at your essays—start with your family and friends, then show them to some colleagues who have already been through business school. Be prepared for their comments. Remember, it's better to hear something negative from them first than to have an admissions committee get the same impression without you having a chance to rectify it. After you get everyone's comments, it's back to the drawing board to revise further.

Month Two

You probably feel as if you're juggling quite a lot at this point, and you're right. Now's the time to start putting it all together. In month two, gather your recommendations. Make sure that your have copies of your transcripts ready to submit. Finalize application forms, and write out checks to accompany the applications. Make sure that you have filled out all of the appropriate financial aid forms. Be sure you have enough copies of your resume if you need to submit them with your applications. Go through each application again, ensuring that you have all the materials that the program has requested. *Finish your essays.*

Month One

You've made it! Now it's time to send in your materials. Review everything one last time for neatness and accuracy. *Make sure you are sending the correct application materials to each program.* Submit your applications, and relax. You deserve it!

If you've had more than one job, ask someone from each workplace to write a recommendation. If there are gaps in your resume or transcript, have one of your recommenders address those gaps.

THE OUTCOME

Don't rest on your laurels for too long, though. After you submit the applications materials, follow up in a week or two to make sure that each program has received everything they need. Do not make a nuisance of yourself; once you have acknowledged that all materials have been received, do not pester admissions personnel about the status of your application. If it's not required by the program, see if you can schedule an interview with admissions personnel. Refer back to Chapter 4 for interviewing tips before you go on any interviews.

Once you receive notices of acceptance, you're still not all the way home. Review financial aid awards, and begin the process of taking out a private loan if that's necessary. See Chapter 5 and Appendix II for information about good sources of private loans.

If you're really lucky, you've been accepted by every business program to which you've applied. Congratulations! Now all you have to do is decide where to go. . .

Resources

BOOKS

General Information about Graduate School and Business School

Bunch, Rick, et al. *Grey Pinstripes with Green Ties: MBA Programs Where the Environment Matters* (World Resources Institute, 1998).

Carpenter, Rebecca O. *Canadian Business Guide to MBA and Executive MBA Programs* (John Wiley & Sons, 1999).

Distance Learning Programs 2000 (Peterson's, 1999).

Finkle, Jane, ed. *Graduate School: The Best Resources to Help You Choose, Get In, and Pay* (Resource Pathways, 1998).

MBA Distance Learning Programs (Peterson's, 1999).

MBA Programs 2000 (Peterson's, 1999).

Mitchell, Lesli. *The Ultimate Grad School Survival Guide* (Peterson's, 1996).

Sherril, Jan-Mitchell, and Craig A. Hardesty. *The Gay, Lesbian, and Bisexual Students' Guide to Colleges, Universities, and Graduate Schools* (New York University Press, 1994).

Personality and Career Assessment

Barrett, James. *Careers, Aptitude and Selection Tests* (Kogan Page Ltd., 1998).

Barrett, James, with Geoff Williams. *Test Your Own Job Aptitude: Exploring Your Career Potential* (Penguin USA, 1995).

Bolles, Richard Nelson. *What Color Is Your Parachute? 2000* (Ten Speed Press, 1999).

Helfand, David P. *Career Change: Everything You Need to Know to Meet New Challenges and Take Control of Your Career* (VGM Career Horizons, 1999).

Janda, Louis H. *Career Tests: 25 Revealing Self-Tests to Help You Find and Succeed at the Perfect Career* (Adams Media Corp., 1999).

Nardi, Dario. *Character and Personality Type: Discovering Your Uniqueness for Career and Relationship Success* (Telos Publications, 2000).

GMAT and TOEFL

GMAT CAT Sucess 2000 (Peterson's, 1999).

Logic & Reading Review for the GRE, GMAT, LSAT, MCAT (Peterson's, 1999).

Math Review for the GRE, GMAT and MCAT (Peterson's, 2000)

Rogers, Bruce. *TOEFL Practice Tests 2000* (Peterson's, 1999).

___. *TOEFL Sucess 2000* (Peterson's, 1999).

Applying to Business School

McClain, Molly, and Jacqueline D. Roth. *Shaum's Quick Guide to Writing Great Essays* (McGraw-Hill, 1998).

Montauk, Richard. *How to Get into the Top M.B.A. Programs* (Prentice-Hall, 1997).

Princeton Language Institute. *21st Century Grammar Handbook*, edited by Joseph Holland (Dell Publishing, 1993).

Stelzer, Richard J. *How to Write a Winning Personal Statement for Graduate and Professional School* (Peterson's, 1997).

Financial Aid

Annual Register of Grant Support 2000: A Directory of Funding Sources (R.R. Bowker, 1999).

Astor, Bart. *The Official Guide to Financing Your MBA*, 2nd ed. (Graduate Management Admission Council, 1994).

Beckham, Barry. *The Black Student's Guide to Scholarships*, 4th ed. (Madison Books, 1996).

College Money Handbook (Peterson's, 1999). *Grants for Graduate & Postdoctoral Study* (Peterson's, 1998).

Insider's Guide to Paying for College (Peterson's, 1999).

McWade, Patricia. *Financing Graduate School* (Peterson's, 1996).

Schlachter, Gail Ann. *Directory of Financial AIDS for Women, 1999–2001* (Reference Service Press, 1999).

Schlachter, Gail Ann, and R. David Weber. *Financial Aid for African Americans 1999–2001* (Reference Service Press, 1999).

___. *Financial Aid for Native American 1999–2001* (Reference Services Press, 1999.

___. *Financial Aid for Veterans, Military Personnel, and Their Dependents: 1998–2000* (Reference Services Press, 1998).

___. *How to Find Out about Financial Aid and Funding: A Guide to Print, Electronic, and Internet Resources Listing Scholarships, Fellowships, Loans, Grants, Awards, and Internships* (Reference Service Press, 1999).

Schlachter, Gail Ann, et al. *Financial Aid for Asian Americans 1999–2001* (Reference Service Press, 1999).

___. *Financial Aid for Hispanic Americans, 1999-2001* (Reference Service Press, 1999).

Scholarship Almanac 2000 (Peterson's, 1999)

Scholarships and Loans for Adult Students (Peterson's, 1999).

Scholarships for Study in the USA and Canada (Peterson's, 1999).

Scholarships, Grants & Prizes 2000 (Peterson's 1999)

ON THE WEB

General Information about Graduate School and Business School

About.com (business majors), businessmajors/about.com/education/businessmajors

American Council on Education, www.acenet.edu

Association for Support of Graduate Students, www.asgs.org

Bschool.com (general information and advice), www.bschool.com

Bureau of Labor Statistics, www.bls.gov

Chronicle of Higher Education, www.chronicle.com

Council of Graduate Schools, www.cgsnet.org

Digest of Education Statistics 1997, www.nces.ed.gov/pubs/digest97

Graduate Management Admission Council, www.gmat.org

The International Association for Management Education, www.aacsb.edu

MBAinfo.com (advice and information-gathering), www.mbainfo.com

MBA Plaza (advice and information-gathering), www.MBAPlaza.com

National Black MBA Association, Washington, D.C., chapter, www.dcbmbaa.org

Peterson's Education Center, www.petersons.com

U.S. Census Bureau, www.census.gov

U.S. Department of Education, www.ed.gov

GMAT and TOEFL

Graduate Management Admission Council, www.gmat.org

Educational Testing Service, www.toefl.org

Applying to Business School

GradAdvantage, www.gradadvantage.org

Financial Aid

Access Group, www.accessgroup.org

Citibank, www.studentloan.com

Consumer Credit Counseling Service, www.nfcc.org

eStudentLoan.com (compare student loans and apply online), www.estudentloan.com

FAFSA on the Web, www.fafsa.ed.gov

FastWeb (online searchable database of aid), www.fastweb.com

FinAid (information and advice), www.finaid.org

International Education Finance Corporation, www.IEFC.com

International Education Financial Aid, www.IEFA.org

National Association of Student Financial Aid Administrators, www.nasfaa.org

Project EASI (information and advice), www.easi.ed.gov

Saludos Web Education Center (aid targeted to Hispanic Americans), www.saludos.com

PROFESSIONAL ORGANIZATIONS

American Accounting Association
5717 Bessie Drive
Sarasota, Florida 34233-2399
Telephone: 813-921-7747
Web site: www.aaa-edu.org

American Association of University Women
1111 16th Street, NW
Washington, DC 20036
Telephone: 202-785-7700
Web site: www.aauw.org

American Business Women's Association
9100 Ward Parkway
P.O. Box 8728
Kansas City, Missouri 64114
Telephone: 816-361-6621
Web site: www.abwahq.org

American Indian Graduate Center
4520 Montgomery Boulevard, NE, Suite 1-B
Albuquerque, New Mexico 87109
Telephone: 505-881-4584
Web site: www.aigc.com

American Institute of Certified Public Accountants
1211 Avenue of the Americas
New York, New York 10036
Telephone: 212-596-6200
Web site: www.aicpa.org

American Management Association
135 West 50th Street
New York, New York 10020-1201
Telephone: 212-586-8100
Web site: www.amanet.org

American Marketing Association
250 South Wacker Drive, Suite 200
Chicago, Illinois 60606
Telephone: 312-648-0536
Web site: www.ama.org

Association for the Support of Graduate Students
P.O. Box 4698
Incline Village, Nevada 89450-4698
Telephone: 775-831-1399
Web site: www.asgs.org

Business and Professional Women
2012 Massachusetts Avenue, NW
Washington, DC 20036
Telephone: 202-293-1100
Web site: www.bpwusa.org

Consortium for Graduate Study in Management
200 South Hanley Road, Suite 1102
St. Louis, Missouri 63015
Web site: www.olin.wustl.edu:8010

Council of Graduate Schools
One Dupont Circle, NW
Washington, DC 20036-1173
Telephone: 202-223-3791
Web site: www.cgsnet.org

Educational Testing Service
P.O. Box 6103
Princeton, New Jersey 08541
Telephone: 609-771-7330
Web site: www.ets.org

Federal Student Aid Information Center
P.O. Box 84
Washington, DC 20044
Telephone: 800-4-FED-AID (toll-free)
Web site: www.ed.gov/prog_info/SFA/StudentGuide

National Association of Graduate-Professional Students
825 Green Bay Road, Suite 270
Wilmette, Illinois 60091
Telephone: 888-88-NAGPS (toll-free)
Web site: www.nagps.org

National Black MBA Association
180 North Michigan Avenue, Suite 1515
Chicago, Illinois 60601
Telephone: 312-236-2622

National Board for Certified Counselors
3 Terrace Way, Suite D
Greensboro, North Carolina 27403-3660
Telephone: 800-398-5389
Web site:www.nbcc.org

National Hispanic Scholarship Fund
P.O. Box 728
Novato, California 94948
Telephone: 415-892-9971
Web site: www.hsf.net

National Society of Public Accountants
1010 North Fairfax Street
Alexandria, Virginia 22314-1574
Telephone: 703-549-6400

Native American Scholarship Fund
8200 Mountain Road, NE, No. 203
Albuquerque, New Mexico 87110-7835
Telephone: 505-262-2351
Web site: www.nasf.com

Project EASI (Easy Access for Students and Institutions)
U.S. Department of Education
600 Independence Avenue ROB-3, Room 5102
Washington, DC 20202
Telephone: 202-708-8391
Web site: www.easi.ed.gov

ACCREDITING AGENCIES

Distance Education and Training Council
1601 Eighteenth Street, NW
Washington, DC 20009
Telephone: 202-234-5100
Web site: www.detc.org

Middle States Association of Colleges and Schools
3624 Market Street
Philadelphia, Pennsylvania 19104
Telephone: 215-662-5606
Web site: www.mscache.org
Accredits institutions in Delaware, District of Columbia, Maryland, New Jersey, New York, Pennsylvania, Puerto Rico, and the Virgin Islands.

New England Association of Schools and Colleges
209 Burlington Road
Bedford, Massachusetts 01730
Telephone: 781-271-0022
Web site: www.neasc.org
Accredits institutions in Connecticut, Maine, Massachusetts, New Hampshire, Rhode Island, and Vermont.

North Central Association of Colleges and Schools
30 North LaSalle, Suite 2400
Chicago, Illinois 60602
Telephone: 800-621-7440
Web site: www.ncacihe.org
Accredits institutions in Arizona, Arkansas, Colorado, Illinois, Indiana, Iowa, Kansas, Michigan, Minnesota, Missouri, Nebraska, New Mexico, North Dakota, Ohio, Oklahoma, South Dakota, West Virginia, Wisconsin, and Wyoming.

Northwest Association of Schools and Colleges
1910 University Drive
Boise, Idaho 83725
Telephone: 208-334-3210
Web site: www2.idbsu.edu/nasc
Accredits institutions in Alaska, Idaho, Montana, Nevada, Oregon, Utah, and Washington.

Southern Association of Colleges and Schools
1866 Southern Lane
Decatur, Georgia 30033
Telephone: 404-679-4500
Web site: www.sacscoc.org
Accredits institutions in Alabama, Florida, Georgia, Kentucky, Louisiana, Mississippi, North Carolina, South Carolina, Tennessee, Texas, and Virginia.

Western Association of Schools and Colleges
985 Atlantic Avenue, Suite 100
Alameda, California 95401
Telephone: 510-632-5000
Web site: www.wascweb.org
Accredits institutions in California, Guam, and Hawaii.

CREDIT REPORTING AGENCIES

Equifax
   P.O. Box 740241
   Atlanta, Georgia 30374
   Telephone: 800-997-2493 (toll-free)
   Web site: www.equifax.com

Experian (formerly TRW)
   P.O. Box 2104
   Allen, Texas 75012
   Telephone: 800-422-4879 (toll-free)
   Web site: www.experian.com

TransUnion
   P.O. Box 390
   Springfield, Pennsylvania 19064
   Telephone: 800-888-4213 (toll-free)
   Web site: www.tuc.com